Crazy Culture

The Sins of Civilization

Peter Heinegg

UNIVERSITY PRESS OF AMERICA,® INC.
Lanham • Boulder • New York • Toronto • Plymouth, UK

Copyright © 2012 by
University Press of America,® Inc.
4501 Forbes Boulevard
Suite 200
Lanham, Maryland 20706
UPA Acquisitions Department (301) 459-3366

Estover Road
Plymouth PL6 7PY
United Kingdom

Library of Congress Control Number: 2011935744
ISBN: 978-0-7618-5683-2 (paperback : alk. paper)
eISBN: 978-0-7618-5684-9

to Gene Tonry,
a trusty guide for the long haul

And Cain knew his wife; and she conceived, and bare Enoch: and he builded a city, and called the name of the city Enoch, after the name of his son, Enoch.

Genesis 4.17

Wenn ich "Kultur" höre, entsichere ich meinen Browning.

Hanns Johst, *Schlageter* (1933)

Contents

Prelude

[P]assions can be contrary to reason only so far as they are accompany'd with some judgment or opinion. According to this principle, which is so obvious and natural, 'tis only in two senses, that any affection can be call'd unreasonable. First, when a passion, such as hope or fear, grief or joy, despair or security, is founded on the supposition or the existence of objects, which really do not exist. Secondly, when in exerting any passion in action, we chuse means insufficient for the design'd end, and deceive ourselves in our judgment of causes and effects. Where a passion is neither founded on false suppositions, nor chuses means insufficient for the end, the understanding can neither justify nor condemn it. 'Tis not contrary to reason to prefer the destruction of the whole world to the scratching of my finger. 'Tis not contrary to reason for me to choose my total ruin, to prevent the least uneasiness of an Indian or person wholly unknown to me. 'Tis as little contrary to reason to prefer even my own acknowledged lesser good to my greater, and have a more ardent affection for the former than the latter.

—David Hume, *A Treatise of Human Nature* (1739-40)

It's true: the key to life is id.
And reason? Logic? Let's not kid
ourselves; the brain's an instrument
for getting stuff that we're intent
on having. Why? Well, just because:
desire has its own weird laws,
no one more strictly rational
than all the rest. We're passional—
like everything in nature's realm,
blind striving firmly aims our helm.

And that explains why earth is doomed:
Since natural selection's groomed
us for survival, *coûte que coûte,*
here's what you get: a cunning brute,
not pretty and without much skill,
except to kill—and then breed still
more killers and breeders: we call
that "culture," "civ'lization";
for beasts it's an abomination:
We slaughter everything that moves
with wings or fins or feet or hooves.
We eat their flesh and wear their skin,
enslave them, even though they're kin.
We make them plow and pull and haul,
we lock them into pen and stall.
we steal their milk and eggs and toil,
we grind their bones to feed our soil.

That's just for starters, then we slash
the forests down, burn trees to ash;
bulldozers help to rape *la terre,*
pollute the waters, foul the air.
Man, this is *easy*! Next in line,
we do the same to humankind:
so women, children, strangers will
be grist for our Satanic mill.

Now one more thing that we need here:
some nonsense for the folks to cheer:
Our Leader, Prophet, Alpha Male
in heaven (and on earth), all hail!
Of course, it's all projection—"HE"
(the Lord of faith's phallocracy)
is just a man in god's disguise,
a childish myth of timeless lies.
He makes the rules, our "mighty king,"
which have that old familiar ring:
"Make babies, dominate the earth,
fight infidels for all you're worth.
And not to worry, once you've screwed
up everything but good, I'll shrewd-
ly nod and bid the angels blow
their horns to launch the Judgment Show.
Ta-DA! And then—you know the drill—
the blood and guts and tears will spill.
I'll kiss or curse you, one-two-three,

then off to (yawn) eternity.
Now as for earth … What earth? Don't bother.
It's toast, who cares?" Thus spake the Father.

Bull-*shit*! Meanwhile, back at the ranch
of Mother Earth no "God" will stanch
the wounds inflicted by our side
("Man" hyperactive, beady-eyed).
Short-sighted lumps, they kill and breed
with wild abandon, since, as needed, "reason" always will produce
the motives, rationales, excuse-
s to fuel the id, our dear old friend,
to pony up the cash to spend
on waste and crime, to fabricate
a storyboard for our sick fate

Thanks, David Hume, our skeptic master.
for shedding light on this disaster,
i.e., on history's ghastly spell,
And Darwin too, and Freud as well:
they showed us how life really works,
why humans must be classed as jerks
(not monsters), whom you can't just fix
with prayer or jail, or self-help tricks.
They're apes with nukes, or crocs with bomb-
s—and big, big dreams, and *there's* the harm.
An *animal rationale*
that swims from Dover to Calais—
and *then* builds concentration camps,
collects fresh scalps along with stamps,
designs utopias—and hells,
likes both to dig and poison wells.
Man plots and schemes, he risks and gambles,
and winds up with—what else?—a shambles.
However daft his misconceptions,
his "reason" will have no objections.
And id's best bud, the human brain,
will underwrite a world of pain.

Too dark a picture for you here?
It's all too true, the record's clear:
You need more data to be sure?
Just come on board this rapid tour
of worthless, crazy, sick *Kultur*

—Peter Heinegg, 2009

Introduction

Everybody loves culture. Well, most people love *their* culture. They cheer for their nation, their tribe, their clan, their gods, their town, their team, their school, their leaders, their heroes, their holy books, their faith, and all their favorite cultural stuff: songs, stories, systems, images, fictions, lies. It's always been this way and always will be. But it's doubtful that culture, the word, the concept, the shibboleth, has ever been more hailed and revered than it is today. Even as more and more of the world's cultures and languages slide toward extinction (with something like 3,000 languages fated to disappear by 2100), ground into the dust by globalism, assimilation, industrialization, genocide, and other unstoppable forces, culture itself becomes increasingly sacred.

We're all multiculturalists now (as Nathan Glazer told us back in 1997); and thank heaven for that. Twenty-first century America, for example, is a far more colorful place than it used to be, and not just because of the welcome, if belated, breakthroughs for women, blacks, gays, and other minorities. In this sports-worshiping country the NBA, the NHL, and major league baseball are awash in foreign players. Supermarket shelves overflow with items unseen and unimagined a generation ago: hummus, feta, radicchio, bok choy, and salsa (now outselling ketchup). Back in the white-bread Eisenhower years, who knew about feng shui, dashikis, gamelans, acupuncture, Bollywood, or Rastafarianism? The gamut of ethnic restaurants in heartland towns used to run from Chinese to Italian; now even in dullish burgs one can find Indian, Japanese, Vietnamese, Thai, Mexican, Jamaican, and everything else under the sun. (There's no avoiding the impression that for most Americans multi-culturalism means going out to eat.)

As with multiculturalism, so with its broader corollary, diversity. The faces we see on TV nowadays, like the ones in our classrooms (on both sides of the desk or lectern), at the gas station, the movies, the motel, and the mall are a refreshingly varied lot. One iconic-comic symbol of this internationalization might be the arrival on *The Simpsons* of Apu, the affable Indian computer science Ph.D. (voiced by a Greek-American Jew, Hank Azaria) and workaholic proprietor of the Springfield Quik-E-Mart. And then—hurrah!—there's our half-Kenyan president.

So far, so good. But there's another brand of multiculturalism making the rounds these days, especially in Academe; and it's been proclaiming a fair share of nonsense. This variety has been handily defined by Penn State's Christopher Clausen in *Faded Mosaic: The Emergence of Post-Cultural America* (2000) as "the multiculturalism of strong ethnic values and group solidarity maintained heroically against the pressures of a Eurocentric majority." In other words, *because* white westerners oppressed, dispossessed, and despised a whole range of "primitive" or "alien" peoples (Amerindians, Africans, "Orientals," Muslims, etc.), those peoples and their cultural products are now ipso facto deserving of our awed admiration and unstinting approval. Clausen cites a news report from 1998 when the San Francisco school board announced its plan to require that at least half the books assigned to high school students be by "authors of color" (no mention of any other standards, except non-whiteness). And then there was the notorious campaign in the late 1990s by the Makah Nation of Washington State to fight cultural genocide by reviving their ancient custom of killing gray whales. (Unfortunately, they had lost all their harpooning skills and had to resort to an elephant gun (.460 caliber); the result wasn't pretty.)

Such instances could easily be multiplied (cf. the wacky "Afro-centrist" claim that much of classical Greek culture was "stolen" from Egypt, or the dewy inspirational fantasies about American Indians by pop-anthropologists like Carlos Castaneda, Lynn Andrews, Derrick Jensen or—yipes!—Ward Churchill). Clausen cites the infamous case of People v. Chen (1989), where a Chinese husband who beat his wife to death with a claw-hammer was let off with probation because of mitigating "cultural" circumstance. (For details, see http://www.princeton.edu/~lawjourn/Spring98/ferraro.html.) Follies of this kind rest on a naive blindness to a feature of all human culture that, for lack of a more scientific term, one could call sinfulness: Every human artifact is fashioned by creatures steeped in egotism and violence, and has to be viewed with a sharp, skeptical eye. As Gerard Manley Hopkins famously wrote in "God's Grandeur" about the pollution and filth of Victorian England:

Generations have trod, have trod, have trod;
And all is seared with trade; bleared, smeared with toil,
And wears man's smudge and shares man's smell.

To put it simply, there's no such thing as an innocent culture. All cultures tend to divide the world into "us" and "them." Historically, all cultures have repressed women, and most have glorified murderous male warriors. Cultures institutionalize cruelty (initiation rites, mutilations, privileged classes, lower castes, marginalization of weaker members, executions, etc.) All cultures damage the environment to some extent—check out the current industrial ecocide in China and the natural gas industry's "fracking" of America. If the vegetarians are right, every time humans eat meat, they're collaborating with and condoning the obscene conditions under which most domesticated birds and animals are raised and slaughtered. All cultures idealize and lie about their origins and golden ages. Maybe Pascal went too far when he cried out that, "The heart of man is hollow and full of ordure" (*Pensées* II, 143), but he had a point.

And it's a point that the starry-eyed votaries of multiculturalism need to recall—at the risk of falling into absurdity. This whole field is booby-trapped with controversial issues; but there's always room for rational evaluation in the light of the hoary old principle that two wrongs don't make a right. Many American blacks nowadays like to take Muslim names as a way of protesting against our country's terrible slaveholding past; but, as historian Ronald Segal reminds us in *Islam's Black Slaves* (2002), over the centuries Arab Muslims have enslaved some 16,000,000 blacks (and slavery still flourishes in places like Mauritania and Nigeria) . Still on the topic of Islam, American leftists, disgusted by right-wing, racist demoniza-tion of Muslims and appalled by Israeli mistreatment of the Palestinians, are all too often willing to ignore crimes like the genocide in Darfur , the dreadful rates of clitoridectomy (and other modes of misogyny) in many Muslim cultures, as well as the endemic anti-Semitism in Arab countries (where *The Protocols of the Elders of Zion* is a perennial best-seller; see Martin Gilbert, *In Ishmael's House* [2010]).

Elsewhere, the spread of misguided political correctness continues apace. *Because* women (and especially women of color) have been shunted aside for so long, high school and college students are now informed that the works of second-rate writers like Kate Chopin or downright mediocre ones like Nikki Giovanni are precious, if not imperishable masterpieces. No fair-minded person can deny that the western canon, even at its greatest, from Homer and Shakespeare to Tolstoy and Yeats, bears the bloody fingerprints of arrogant male chauvinism—but that in itself doesn't turn Aphra Behn or Elizabeth Barrett Browning or Harper Lee into world-class artists. Being right (sympa-thetic to the downtrodden, etc.) doesn't automatically make you worthy of ap-plause, or else the following lines by an anonymous 19th-century anti-slavery poet quoted in *The Stuffed Owl* would be great literature:

Why streams the life-blood from that female throat?
She sprinkled gravy on a guest's new coat.

And then there's the ticklish problem of affirmative action. With nepotism and the old-boy network theoretically banned (but still functioning), with openly advertised and transparently conducted job searches now the law, we would all like to think that recruiting is fairer than it used to be. But there's a lot of anecdotal evidence (see Mary Lefkowitz, *History Lessons: A Race Odyssey*, 2008) that in their effort to atone for the injuries of the past, college administrators—to take one instance—sometimes hire and promote under-qualified minorities. Hiring has always been a chancy affair, and absolute meritocracy an unreachable dream. But if deans and presidents in bygone days had their own narrow agendas, they at least avoided the unctuous, self-congratulatory tone one hears from their descendants when they score an affirmative action "coup"—even if they had to downplay pointy-headed intellectual qualifications to do it. All job appointments are a long-term wager; so perhaps all one can ask of employers is the admission that they're hoping their bet works out. The old fogies occasionally hired incompetents; the young Turks will too. It happens.

The bottom line to all the swirling arguments and outcries over multiculturalism is, as Clausen emphatically maintains, that culture in the traditional, "thick" sense is by and large passé. That is, the norms, role models, and prescriptions of all sorts that have been handed down from elders to the young can no longer be accepted and followed just by virtue of their being "our way." Of course, such a dictum would strike most Americans as self-evident. The central metaphor for modern life is the supermarket: As soon as you're old enough, *you* decide what cultural stuff—what sort of politics, religion, sexuality, education, and (Lord help us) "lifestyle"—*you* want to buy. Any other system would be un-American. (Yes, there are a few quaint little communities where old-fashioned culture rules: Old Order Amish, Lubavitchers, FLDS polygamists, recent Muslim immigrants, and perhaps a dwindling cluster of Pueblo Indians; but *we* can scarcely imagine living like that.)

Americans don't realize how subversive all this is. "Freedom to choose" isn't just a code-word for abortion. It's a death sentence for many of the old ways. Even if—as proverbially happens, or used to happen, with young couples once they have children—one feels driven to go back to one's "roots" (assuming such roots are findable, viable, and non-toxic), the fact that the individual is the one selecting the beliefs and practices that seem best to him or her transports us into the "post-cultural" realm for good. When you pay for something, you own it (thought it may also wind up owning you). And if you don't like it, you can always throw it away or bring it back to the store and exchange it for something else. The customer is king.

This isn't necessarily a happy state of affairs. If cultural groups are deeply fallible, so are private persons. The culture of the marketplace has created a rootless, ignorant, narcissistic populace (devoted to what Clausen calls "mass individualism"), glued to the tube, mostly unaware of the past, with next to no sense of ceremony or songs, stories, and wisdom known "by heart," consumerists rather than communicants. Almost 200 years ago, that shrewd aristocrat Alexis de Tocqueville delivered a withering assessment of this new pattern of life when he wrote of "an innumerable multitude of men, all equal and alike, incessantly endeavoring to procure the petty and paltry pleasures with which they glut their lives" (*Democracy in America,* 1835, tr. Henry Reeves). And he hadn't seen eBay or *The Price is Right.*

To be sure, what goes on in this hectic 24/7 melting pot (the alternative salad bowl metaphor hasn't worn so well) is culture too, since in one way or another, we can't carry on without cultural software connected to our genetic hard drives. Compared with some of the cultures of the past (10th century Córdoba, medieval Esfahan, Renaissance Italy, Elizabethan England), it's a rather pathetic show. But there's no going back to palmier cultural days (that's what museums and libraries are for), since we don't want to re-adopt the countless mistakes of the past. Above all, we can't surrender our right to judge the pros and cons of everything cultures do and say. Nowadays who could echo Stephen Decatur's "our country, right or wrong" without a snicker or a blush? Apart, that is, from our 50 million or so registered Republicans.

"Our age," said Immanuel Kant in the Introduction to *A Critique of Pure Reason* (1781), "is an age of criticism and to criticism everything must submit." So no work of literature, even one about the life of victimized natives (like the epoch-making memoir, *I, Rigoberta Menchú,* which won its author the 1992 Nobel Peace Prize, but turned out to be crammed with fiction), no popular festival, whether established, like the *Día de los Muertos,* or newfangled, like Kwanzaa (whose inventor, Ron Karenga once said, "Jesus was psychotic"), no nostalgic fantasies, such as Revolutionary War re-enactments or Pioneer Days, no custom whatsoever—wearing kirpans (Sikh ornamental swords) or waving Confederate flags or whooping like "savages" to cheer the home team (the NCAA has wisely banned Indian "mascots")—can get a free pass.

Cultural matters always involve imponderable standards of taste—try convincing a old rock fan that Mozart's "*Il core vi dono*" from *Così Fan Tutte* is better than the Rolling Stones' "Satisfaction"; try offering burqas to nudists—but we have to use the tools we have: reason and experience. Multiculturalists, insofar as they believe in cultural relativism, argue that you can't criticize any culture from the outside; and many, if not most, younger Americans would likely agree ("Hey, so long as nobody gets hurt . . ."). But that will never do. We can and should criticize stupidity and untruth and anything that needlessly diminishes humans (and other life forms).

Most Christians, non-Christians, and hard-core atheists can agree that ethical truths aren't personal or tribal, but universal. In Philippians 4.8 Paul provides a handy list of criteria for evaluating culture: "Whatever is true, whatever is honorable, whatever is just, whatever is pure, whatever is commendable, if there is any excellence and there is anything worthy of praise" (RSV). Negatively speaking, whatever violates those canons deserves to be condemned, no matter whose ideological ox is being gored. Jingoism of any stripe, racism and sexism of any persuasion, chauvinistic self-promotion of any kind, must be taboo—even for the best-intentioned multiculuralists. These days when prophets come forward, we have to give them polygraphs. This book will attempt to do just that.

Even before I begin, I'd argue that the case against culture is a slam-dunk. Culture can be defined as everything humans do to the natural world, and nowadays no honest person can doubt that we're on the verge of destroying the planet. Even school children know how: overpopulation, global warming, pollution, destructive agriculture, animal husbandry, mining, and all the other usual suspects are doing us in. See Greg Morrison's illuminating, under-read book *The Spirit in the Gene: Humanity's Proud Illusion and the Laws of Nature* (1999) for a detailed scenario of the coming debacle. Given the catastrophes and horrors we 've recently unleashed, it's fair to claim that culture is already, on the whole, a massive failure, and our habitual glorying in humanity's grand achievements is at worst a vicious lie and at best a childish delusion. All by itself, that wouldn't save anyone's skin; but there might be some value in honestly acknowledging it.

Chapter One

The Primal Sin

Globally, roughly 450 billion land animals are now factory farmed every year. (There is no tally of fish.) Ninety-nine percent of all land animals eaten or used to produce milk and eggs in the United States are factory farmed. So although there are important exceptions, to speak about eating animals today is to speak about factory farming.

—Jonathan Safran Foer, *Eating Animals* (2009)

No one picture could do justice to the cruel absurdities of culture; no one billion pictures could. Still, if I had to pick an example, I'd probably choose one from the batch of photos published in the *New York Times* on May 14, 2010 from the wedding, earlier that January, of South African President Jacob Zuma. The bride Tobeka Madiba, 38 (nearly 30 years younger than her husband), already has three children by him (he has 16 others by four previous wives, and there's apparently a "fiancée" waiting in the wings). As the president's brother, Mike Zuma, told reporters, "This is a traditional affair, and there is a lot of dancing and celebrating. Later we will slaughter some animals and have a feast with the guests." But actually some slaughtering had already taken place, because Zuma and many of his male friends wore leopard pelts on their shoulders; and Zuma himself displayed a leopard-skin head band as he cavorted in a skirt of what looked like fluffy ropes dangling from his capacious gut. And a good time was had by all, except, of course, for the long-dead leopards and the unspecified critters served as entrees.

It sounds like a précis of human history: the most violent and self-serving of all animals butchers a bunch of other animals to wear their skin and eat their flesh; and everybody pats one another on the back. Well, not everybody. Some people have been dismayed or horrified by the spectacle of the human race's behavior. There have been critics, complainers, satirists, and

1

misanthropes, from Ecclesiastes to Xenocrates to Juvenal to Gracián to Swift to Leopardi to Kafka to Beckett and beyond; and, though they hardly form a coherent school, I'd like to salute them. But the fact is, truly pessimistic views of humanity have always been rare (publically espousing them would be political suicide); and many of the harshest assailants of society—Christians, Marxist, and ecologists—have also indulged in dreams of a utopian future, once the evils they attack will have been swept away.

The idea that humans are, *somme toute*, an evolutionary mistake is both hard to conceive and painful to believe, though perhaps it now seems increasingly obvious. The nearly three centuries that have passed since the King of Brobingnag delivered his famous judgment, "I cannot but conclude the bulk of your natives to be the most pernicious race of little odious vermin that nature ever suffered to crawl upon the face of the earth" have only strengthened his case. And in our own context here, I.B. Singer's dictum, "In relation to [animals] all people are Nazis; for the animals it is an eternal Treblinka," looks more or less axiomatic.

There really isn't much room for argument on this one. As far back as Upton Sinclair's *The Jungle* (1906), but picking up speed and resonance, from Peter Singer's *Animal Liberation* (1975) to Jonathan Safran Foer's *Eating Animals* (2009), generations of thinkers, reporters, and advocates have made it absolutely clear that the overwhelming majority of meat, fish, eggs, and dairy products in this country (and elsewhere) come out of a vast system of torture and misery; and that, given all the cost constraints, this won't change any time soon. (For a quick, stomach-turning *amuse-gueule,* check out a few videos under "animal cruelty" and "factoring farming" on Youtube.)

In restaurants and dining rooms, cafeterias and snack bars, work places and play spaces, across the land, three and more times a day generally overweight men, women, and children stuff themselves with billions of pounds of previously mistreated and tormented animal corpses ("prepared" far from potentially grossed-out consumers' eyes). We call that American cuisine, although the equivalent is available almost everywhere.

Of course, before we could set up our archipelago of holding pens and death camps, we had to take over the whole biome, which we did in record time, killing most of the wild animals (bye-bye, bison) on it, especially the predators (the now extinct California grizzly emblazoned on the state flag, the wolves, the big cats, etc.), whacking the forests, plowing the plains, damming the rivers, lopping off the mountain tops, paving over the land, and spilling three hundred million people every which way. It's how the West, and every other part of the US, was "won," although there's little uniquely American about it all, except maybe the speed. And it's a lot worse in a lot of other places, given our late start. We are, after all, one of the least densely populated nations on earth, far behind Bangladesh, India and Japan, though ahead of Australia, Mongolia, and Greenland.

But, humanly crowded as America now is (compared with the past), none of us saw this process unfold, any more than we watched our previously breathing dinner get slaughtered, skinned, hacked and packed. The one kind of butchery we've all witnessed—and in many instances personally caused—is the hecatomb of animals run over on our roads and streets. Wikipedia (google "road kill") cites one Merritt Clifton for the estimate in any given year something like 41 million squirrels, 26 million cats, 22 million rats, 19 million opossums, 15 million raccoons, 6 million dogs and 350,000 deer are crunched into oblivion. Then there are the countless snakes, frogs, birds, and insects. Birds by the billions likewise come to grief from power lines, radio-transmission, TV, and cell phone towers, oversize windows, acid rain insecticide and feral cats (see Alan Weisman, *The World Without Us*).

Not that it bothers us for long—that's the beauty of myopia. Not many people reflect on the bloody reality behind the leather shoes and boots and belts and gloves and jackets we wear (or the upholstery we sit on), behind the menus we scan day after day, the tens of millions of cookbooks and foodie magazines we buy every year. Some forms of animal exploitation, as seen, say, in the making of foie gras or fur coats, have become less common; but what about those towering islands of pet food bags and cans (for our 68 million dogs and 73 million cats) in our supermarkets? On the other hand, circuses, rodeos, zoos and animal acts, while modifying some of their worst practices, continue to mistreat and exploit their prisoners for company profits and audience amusement.

What all this comes down to is the consequence of the age-old belief that we are the center of the universe, which was either carefully crafted by God for our benefit or else just cleverly hijacked by a long line of inventers, entrepreneurs, and adventurers, who can now do almost everything the old Creator could, except live forever. In any case, as our spectacular consumption of our fellow beasts makes plain—and let's not forget the vast ongoing annihilation of laboratory animals (100 million a year in the US? it's hard to keep track), most of them for useless, redundant "research"—we *are* in charge; we feel perfectly comfortable being in charge; and we can't conceive any other way of doing things. It's our culture.

Yes, attitudes are changing. Animal rights are gaining more recognition. Pet owners are now sometimes called "guardians." Cruelty to animals receives harsher penalties, including the odd prison sentence. Movie credits flash possibly credible announcements that "No animals were harmed in the making of this film." Vegetarianism and veganism are becoming more widespread; e.g., most restaurants now post one non-meat entrée. The mildly educational "Animal

Planet" cable channel is quite popular. The much-mocked PETA seems to be going strong. Writers like Peter Singer, Michael Pollan, Erik Markus, etc. are making their voices heard. And so on.

But all that doesn't really amount to much. First, much of the damage is already done and irreparable, like the extinction of the passenger pigeon and the drowning of Hetch Hetchy Valley and Glen Canyon. The population of America has nowhere to go but up; and all those people need and demand more space, food, and water. (When coyotes or cougars trot into the suburbs, we know how *that*'s going to end.) More factory farms, more coal mines and oil and gas wells, more highways, giant feedlots and piggeries and chicken and turkey farms, landfills, gated communities, prisons, mega-churches, stadiums, and so forth—it's in the cards.

All this mass of humanity will require more animal products, more beef, veal, pork, poultry, and that other dietary euphemism, "seafood," discreetly dressed, plastic-wrapped and ready for the oven, frying pan or barbecue grill. And the only economic way to keep providing that Himalaya of bloody flesh will be the market-honed methods of agribusiness: keeping vast herds and flocks of animals in near-immobility, shooting them as full of hormones as possible, fattening them as fast as possible, and killing them as soon as possible. It's not pretty; but it's a sight almost no one ever sees (or wants to), and it *works*. Meat is cheap, and it tastes good: end of story.

There's no reasonable hope of countering the forces of evolution that got us where we are today. Humans, like all other creatures, are programmed to seek pleasure without taking too many risks; and meat offers a whole range of delicious smells, textures, and flavors that *homo sapiens* and his ancestors have delighted in for millions of years; so why should they change their m.o. now? The only danger appears to be an overdose of cholesterol, charcoal, or fat here or there; but we can work that out.

And, despite the many different patterns in agriculture and food consumption between America and other nations, the overall picture is almost uniformly bad. As Mark Bittman points out in "Rethinking the Meat-Guzzler" (*New York Times*, January 27, 2008), in 1961 the world's meat supply was 71 million tons; by 2007 it was 284 million tons. One of the surest measures of national wealth is per capita meat consumption; and as China, India, and other once-poor countries climb toward the good life, they'll doubtless spend more and more of their money on meat. Commercial fisheries may collapse, as many experts predict, by the middle of this century; but the ecological disaster of pisciculture will linger and spread.

And why not? It's our world, damn it—this land is your land, this land is my land, from American Samoa to the U.S. Virgin Islands. "And God said, 'Let us make man in our image, after our likeness: and let them have domination over the fish of the sea, and over the fowl of the air, and over all cattle, and over all the earth, and over every creeping thing that creepeth upon the earth'." Nature writers often flag this passage as the ultimate in anthropocentric arrogance. Fair enough; but what may be more insidious is its effortless logic: Sharing with our imaginary Creator the quasi-divine power of speech, humans see no reason not to use that communicative weapon to take over the planet. The Book of Job bids us feel awe at the sight of war horses, hippos, and crocodiles; but that was long before the invention of AK-47s and WMDs.

We dominate and decimate animals because we can; because it's convenient and pleasurable. A relatively small group of people have to do the behind-the-scenes dirty work in barns and abattoirs and packing plants to funnel that huge supply of animal protein into our houses and onto our tables; but, vile and dangerous as assembly-line butchering is, needy folks—including a host of illegal immigrants—keep turning up to do it. Forget that rarified Buddhist notion of right livelihood: it's a luxury the masses can't afford—not that the elites, bourgeois or otherwise, have ever bothered a whole lot about it either. To ask humans to stop increasing and multiplying (a command God needn't have bothered to issue), to stop expanding into every square inch of available territory, to stop grabbing and consuming whatever they find in front of them—in "their" fields, pastures, mines, and malls—is asking too much.

The primal sin of culture is thus self-centeredness combined with lethal power. Evolution leaves us no alternative to either of these forces, since any creature that didn't see itself at the center of its own field of vision would quickly perish, and power once acquired *will* be used. In principle, rational self-awareness should serve as a check on our ecocidal-suicidal tendencies (as has so far been the case with all-out nuclear war); but everyone knows how weak that rational command-and-control mechanism is. It typically fails to make us postpone immediate gratification (whence widespread crippling debt, addictions, obesity, STDs, unplanned pregnancies, and so forth) and to acknowledge the damage we're doing either to ourselves (with cigarettes, drugs, or alcohol, say), or to the natural world (with strip mining, oil-drilling, or slash-and-burn agriculture).

It's not just the potent lure of pleasure that strings us along, but the crazy myths and fantasies our brains have swathed us in, beginning and ending with the dream of our infinite, eternal, godlike importance. The clearest evidence for this can be found in monotheistic discourse (see Chapter III, "The Religious Sins"), where animals seldom appear except as divinely provided dinner, slaves, or possible sources of ritual uncleanliness. (So far theologians haven't explained why the Lord ever made *tref* animals to begin with.) In the Christian and Muslim (and presumably Jewish) versions of the afterlife, there are no sub-human creatures whatsoever (no wonder, given their obstinate lack of interest in worshipping the Almighty). Dogs, it may be noticed, are spoken of with hostility and disgust throughout the Hebrew Bible. The only pet hound appears in the non-canonical Book of Tobit.

Along those lines, common cultural parlance is happy to vilify the worst sorts of human behavior as "animalistic," including everything catty, fishy, mulish, sheepish, swinish, waspish, wolvish, apelike, snakelike shark-like, or vulpine—whereas all things "humane" are ultra-praiseworthy, thank you. Merely labeling a person with an animal name puts him or her down as an ass, baboon, bat, chicken, cow, cuckoo, dinosaur, goat, goose, hyena, jackal, leech, loon, louse, maggot, parrot, piranha, polecat, rat, shrimp, skunk, sloth, slug, turkey, viper, vulture, weasel, worm, and so on. Rutting males are alley cats or billy goats and may even engage in "bestiality," which generally means raping a beast. The Bible (Lev. 20.15) forthrightly condemns all animal victims of such rape to death.

Even as we degrade animals, no culture, it seems, can spend enough time and effort glorifying its great men (many of them gore-spattered), raising monuments, funerary and otherwise, to its heroes, saints, and favorite sons, naming cities, states, universities, buildings, and airports after them, so everyone can bask in the afterglow. There's no need to list many instances of this pattern, from Alexandria to Zanesville, with the J. Edgar Hoover FBI Building and Oral Roberts U. in the middle, since it's so universal. The bottom line is that all culture is narcissistic—e.g., in July, 2010, as reported in *Harper's Magazine*, when Venezuelan officials exhumed the corpse of Simón Bolívar, President Hugo Chávez tweeted, "My God, my God ... my Christ, our Christ ... This glorious skeleton must be Bolívar because you can feel his presence. My God." More and more people, mostly men, think they deserve to live forever, and so are investing in cryonics. If the gods won't do the job, maybe quack-science can.

Creatures either actually or potentially as great as this—and aren't we all great, in one way or another?—tower over all the lesser animals, who have borne the brunt of our domination forever. Outside the charmed circle of petdom, animal pain does not compute: Having reduced their species and numbers to levels we find convenient, we ignore the suffering caused by separation from their young, confinement, enslavement, torture, sensory deprivation of every kind, and brutal slaughter. We do this because, once again, we can; and it's the primal sin of culture. But it's a sin blessed by immemorial custom (so that practically all family feasts center around the ritual consumption of suitably disguised animal cadavers), approved by God-Yahweh-Allah (as the Creator of all beasts, he generously dishes them up for our delectation), and all-but-invisible (how wise to keep slaughterhouses off-limits to the public).

Major religious celebrations—Christmas, Easter, Thanksgiving, Passover, Rosh Hashanah, Eid al-Adha)—would be unthinkable without their liturgical hecatombs. The Bible doesn't blush to acknowledge that animal sacrifices are meant to substitute for human sacrifice (Ex. 12,21; 13.12.13; etc.) Just give God the blood; and he'll let you eat the rest.

Protesters against this system are tolerated as sentimental eccentrics or mocked as goofy wimps "Vegetarian: Sioux word for poor hunter" reads a bumper sticker on my yobbish neighbor's pickup truck in Schenectady, NY. "Vegetarians," proclaims take-no-prisoners chef Anthony Bourdain in *Kitchen Confidential*, "and their Hezbollah-like splinter faction, the vegans, ... are the enemy of everything good and decent in the human spirit." And rare is the carnivore-philosopher who forgets to remind us that Hitler was a vegetarian, which only goes to show you that ... appearances are deceptive— or something.

At any rate, practically everyone can agree that the flesh and edible products of living creatures taste yummy; and that renouncing them would mean a serious loss of pleasure: Cooked animal bodies pack a delicious wallop, not least of all in America, where meat is disproportionately cheaper than elsewhere. So it's safe to conclude that we can't expect any radical change on this front for a long time (it took the author of these pages, a professed animal-lover, over half a century to come to—or distance himself from— his senses on the subject of eating meat). One might anticipate or hope that America will eventually adopt the EU's modest improvements in "humane" housing and treatment of farm animals (chickens, pigs, veal calves, etc.)

But let's not kid ourselves. By the time that happens, if it happens, we will have already lost more of the world's endangered species—tigers, Amur leopards, mountain gorillas, giant pandas, white and Javan rhinoceroses, polar bears, narwhals, North Pacific right whales, bluefin tuna, hawksbill turtles, and so forth. Hey, we need their space or want their flesh or just don't care. Yes, we'll spend lots of money on our pets; and few of us would personally engage in acts of overt cruelty to any non-threatening live animals whose path we happened to cross. But only posey-sniffers and tree-huggers (two mostly imaginary species, akin to the nearly-non-existent "bra-burners") would argue for paying the price it would take to give animals anything like a decent habitat or a life even faintly resembling their old one. In any case it's too late now—thanks to what we call culture: This land was made for you and me, now come and get it.

Chapter Two

The Sexist Sins

But afterwards Zeus who gathers the clouds said to him (Prometheus) in anger: "Son of Iapetus, surpassing all in cunning, you are glad that you have outwitted me and stolen fire—a great plague to your yourself and to men that shall be. But I will give men as the price for fire an evil thing in which they may all be glad of heart while they embrace their own destruction."

So said the father of men and gods, and laughed aloud. And he bade famous Hephaestus make haste and mix earth with water and put in it the voice and strength of human kind, and to fashion a sweet, lovely maiden-shape, like to the immortal goddesses in face; and Athena to teach her needlework and the weaving of the varied web; and golden Aphrodite to shed grace upon her head and cruel longing and cares that weary the limbs. And he charged Hermes the guide, the Slayer of Argos, to put in her a shameless mind and a deceitful nature.

So he ordered. . . . Forthwith the famous Lame God moulded clay in the likeness of a modest maid . . . And the goddess bright-eyed Athene girded and clothed her, and the divine Graces and queenly Persuasion put necklaces of gold upon her, and the rich-haired Hours crowned her head with spring flowers. And Pallas Athene bedecked her form with all manner of finery. Also the Guide, the Slayer of Argos, contrived within her lies and crafty words and a deceitful nature at the will of loud thundering Zeus, and the Herald of the gods put speech in her. And he called this woman Pandora, because all they who dwelt on Olympus gave each a gift, a plague to men who eat bread.

But when he had finished the sheer, hopeless snare, the Father sent glorious Argos-Slayer, the swift messenger of the gods, to take it to Epimetheus as a gift. And Epimetheus did not think on what Prometheus had said to him, bidding him never to take a gift of Olympian Zeus, but to send it back for fear it might be something harmful to men. But he took the gift, and afterwards, when the evil thing was already his, he understood.

For ere this the tribes of men lived on earth remote and free from ills and hard toil and heavy sicknesses which bring the fates upon men; for in misery men grow old quickly. But the woman took off the great lid of the jar with her hands and scattered all these and her thought caused sorrow and mischief to men.

—Hesiod, *Works and Days*, ll. 53-95, tr. Hugh G. Evelyn-White (1914)

It's an old line, and we all know it: Back in the various Dark Ages things used to be *really* bad for women; but now they've dramatically improved; and in the future, well, the sky's the limit. Once upon a time, strange to say, people *believed* the vicious old myths about Pandora and Eve (and Lilith); but now we're cool. Au contraire, no one could count—and most people just ignore—all the carryovers from the poisoned past that still infect our world today. Of the three thousand or so young women I've taught and met in college classrooms over the last forty years, the vast majority think that the battle for equality is basically over (in their neck of the woods anyway); and that all they need to do now is zoom ahead. Only fogies believe in myths.

In truth, cultural history is by and large misogyny writ large and consecrated in texts, images, institutions, habits, attitudes, etc. On August 1, 2010 newspapers around the country flashed pictures of President Bill Clinton walking down the aisle with a veiled young woman, looking for all the world as if he were participating in one of our most venerable rites: the transfer of a daughter by her father-owner to her husband-owner. Clinton rejected this creepy antiquated notion in advance, saying Chelsea was her own woman (newspapers described him as "escorting" her); but the photo drowned him out. And, God knows, at that very moment (more or less), in countless different places, millions of young woman or girls *were* being legally transferred to their new male owners. Not for nothing does the Hebrew word *ba'al,* like the Greek word *kýrios,* mean both husband and lord. Even the most aggressively egalitarian Shakespearean wife, Lady Macbeth, calls her husband "Gentle my lord" [3.2.27]. The myths live.

That kind of language has more or less vanished; but the violent domination it's based on and reflects has not. No one has reliable statistics on all the beatings and rapes that occur in America and elsewhere every year, since most of them go unreported, but everyone knows the number is sky-high. NOW estimates that a third of all women murdered in America are killed by "intimate partners," and that approximately five million women are assaulted or raped by their i.p.s every year (NOW 2009). As with other crimes, men do it because they can do it, and because their culture allows or ignores it. *Plus ça change . . .*

It seems pretty safe to generalize that all cultures, above and beyond their other noxious doings, have oppressed women, even if guilty multicultural

First-Worlders shrink from damning Third World sexists. Nevertheless, thanks to feminism, misogyny, one of culture's oldest, worst, and most persistent sins, has in recent decades become one that people are acutely aware of. History is literally being rewritten as researchers probe the past—often in vain—for records of woman (and others) hitherto passed over in silence. Of course, self-congratulatory popular versions of this new history continue to claim victory: As in the old Virginia Slims ads, women can now settle back and enjoy the many freedoms graciously granted them, you know, the right to vote and all that other neat stuff.

Unfortunately, as a brief mental flight around the world will show, the past is still with us. The "Findings" column in the March, 2011 issue of *Harper's* reports that, "In India . . . 1.8 million female children were estimated to have died between 1985 and 2005 as an indirect result of domestic violence against their mothers; the boys of abused mothers were not at increased risk of death" (*The Times of India*, January 7, 2011). Like Indians, Chinese and South Korean families show their strong preference for boys by resorting to sex-selective abortion.

Elsewhere, as if to illustrate Virginia Woolf's sarcastic remark in *A Room of One's Own,* that "Publicity in women is detestable. Anonymity runs in their blood. The desire to be veiled still possesses them," millions of Muslim women, both in their home countries and in the Islamic diaspora, still walk about (when they're allowed to walk about) shrouded in the hijab, niqab, or burqa. Their second-class status divinely established by the Qur'an (4:34), such women make do the best they can, even as various loopy liberal defenders of Islam orate about the subtle virtues of female covering. (At times one hears a hinted assumption that without it Muslim males couldn't restrain themselves from assaulting and raping their immodest sisters—after all, a 2008 survey by the Egyptian Group for Women's rights reported that in Egypt 98% of foreign women and 83% of Egyptian women were sexually harassed.) When even the gutless, politically correct UN can issue *"The Arab Human Development Report 2005* (optimistically subtitled *Toward the Rise of Women in the Arab World*) criticizing sexist—and economically suicidal—Muslim labor practices, you know there's a big problem.

And then there's the usual gamut of abuses, naturally not limited to the Muslim world: child-, cousin-, and arranged marriages (premature pregnancies leading to obstetric fistulas, etc.); polygyny, female infanticide, denial of schooling to girls, exclusion of women from the workplace, politics, and public life, wife-beating (universally practiced, but prescribed and praised only by mullahs; see the sermons on Youtube), honor killing, mass rape (from the Russian Army in WWII to Bosnia in the 1990s ,to Congo now), ordinary rape (in a 2009 survey one in four South African males questioned admitted

to raping a woman), murder (see the *feminicidios* in Ciudad Juárez). It's a cul-
tural thing. (All the old heroes did it, e.g., Gilgamesh, Homeric warriors, and
Amir Hamza and his foster-brother Aadi Madi-Karib in the wildly popular
Indo-Persian epic *The Adventures of Amir Hamza*).

The developed world may see less of the above, proportionately, given better
education and legal protection; but it has its own share of crimes, miseries, and
outrages that feminism, once again, keeps drawing our attention to: domestic
violence, female-impoverishment-through divorce, the glass ceiling, the absurd
demands of the supermom myth, unfair division of labor, the continual stereo-
typing and exploitation of women in the media, religion-based misogyny, and
so forth. Culture's toolkit for dominating women boggles the mind.

At the same time, there's no blinking the large amount of enablement and
cooperation with male oppression by the women who are its victims. Even
after discounting the enormous extent to which all this is due to fear, indoctrination, and bribery, any honest observer has to acknowledge the countless
ways that women, after becoming enslaved and objectified, have proceeded
to internalize, often enthusiastically, the masculist traditions demeaning and
degrading them, and to indentify with their masters. Women are the ones who
perform clitoridectomies on helpless girls (see Ousmane Sembène's powerful
film, *Moolaadé* (2004). For centuries rabbis, priests, and imams have taught
women (aka the daughters of Eve) to loathe themselves (e.g., for menstruat-
ing) and accept male domination as God's plan; and for centuries women
have passed that course with flying colors. Woe unto those who didn't.
Almost as much as their out-to-lunch husbands, POSSLQs, and male family
members, American women still fight shy of the dreaded term "feminist."

In another common instance, brow-beaten Catholic women have bowed
to an all-male, quasi-celibate hierarchy that has dictated insane sexual and
reproductive rules, while solemnly forbidding them to be ordained. Many
"women of faith" have humbly accepted their place in a patriarchal harem.
Others have served without complaint as brood mares for their divinely ap-
pointed lords and masters (cf. the latest incarnation of Christian natalism,
the Quiverfull movement). And while politically powerful female believers
(Sarah Palin, Michelle Bachmann, Marsha Blackburn, etc.) have indeliber-
ately (one hopes) used their political power to disempower women, millions
of their loyal nameless sisters have fueled that process, for example by opposing the ERA, clamoring against women's rights, and voting for hyper-con-
servative candidates. And, in keeping with their age-old reluctance to openly
rebel against their oppressors, women have always been slower than men to
embrace atheism and agnosticism, which at least in theory are more welcom-
ing to feminism. (Oh right, there was Madalyn Murray O'Hair, once *Life*
magazine's "most hated woman in America." Unbelief is just not ladylike.)

Religious or not, women absorb the same sexist cultural carcinogens and suffer the same toxic effects from them. If not as homophobic as men—even as they are in general less pugnacious and violently vengeful—women have certainly been led to recite the same heterosexist nonsense as their brothers. Anita Bryant will be forever remembered for mouthing the corny diatribe against "Adam and Steve"; but bigoted Christian women everywhere were with her. Old newsreels show us delirious crowds of women shouting for Hitler or mourning for Stalin, like the recent videos of nuns hailing John Paul II on papal visits or thousands of girl gymnasts ecstatically flipping and female soldiers fiercely marching for Kim Jong Il. Men lead, women cheerlead.

It's a bitter truth to face, and a lot of people would just as soon ignore it. What, do we have to take a knife to our Bibles and Qur'ans? Do we have to rewrite the lives of all our Great Men, from Siddhartha Gautama to Mahatma Gandhi, from Confucius to Jefferson, from Muhammad to Machiavelli to Mao? Do we have to cast a cold eye on all our generals, warlords, and battle-scarred veterans? Yes, yes, and yes. But, unfortunately, we can't just replace the toppled statues of both the Saddam Husseins and our kinder, gentler modern western heroes with unjustly neglected female figures of equal stature—because we don't have nearly enough of them to go round. (Not that hero worship of any kind is a good idea.)

The sad truth (as in Ernest Renan's immortal question, "*Qui sait si la vérité n'est pas triste?*") is that oppression works. A mute, inglorious Milton is by definition not a poet at all. *The American Heritage Dictionary* goes out of its way to use photos of women to illustrate words we more often associate with men, like "hardhat" or "jockey silks." Less reasonably, the editors also provide pictorial listings of all the American First Ladies and their (often quite minor) achievements. (Quick, what's Mrs. Lou Hoover famous for?) But, insofar as this creates an impression of actual equality, it's a distortion. The past is past; and for the most part the bad guys won. In any event, "guys" have controlled the creation, dissemination, and enforcement of culture. And, man, do they have a lot to answer for.

Nietzsche defined life as the will-to-power; and the same is true of cultural life. It is, or has been so far, an ongoing scrum, an interplay of power relationships—alternate kinds of speech, for example, or other modes of self-expression—vying for predominance, relying on or rebelling against others. Thus, styles in everything, from dress to song to sex to government to family structure change and evolve in response to social forces. Consider, for example, the history of romantic love, from the la-dee-da literary conceits of *l'amour courtois* to the more physiologically-psychologically-therapeutically-grounded.contemporary fashions in sexual behavior. Throughout all this process, however, until very recently there's always been, and still is today, a major excess of male power skewing the whole grid, as it did a century and a half ago, in the days of Emma Bovary. The inevitable, obvious, naïve-sounding (but so what?) conclusion is that culture has been bad for women. And even as they were being possessed and controlled, women had only limited opportunities to resist; and in fact mostly just passed on all the bad ideas of the *ancien régime* to their unsuspecting offspring, male and female. The hand the rocked the cradle warped the world. It's extremely hard to break the ties that bind and become a revolutionary. And many revolutions run aground, peter out, or get co-opted.

There's no fair way to get around this—certainly not just by writing and teaching about neglected female figures from the past. That's a worthwhile project, but there are precious few unheralded female geniuses still left out there—most of them were silenced or effectively buried alive. Virginia Woolf wasn't quite accurate when she wondered ironically in *A Room of One's Own* (1929), "It is a perennial puzzle why no woman wrote a word of that extraordinary [Elizabethan] literature when every other man, it seemed, was capable of a song or sonnet." Yes, there were a handful of late 16th and early 17th century British women writers; but none of them was greatly gifted. Undeterred by this paucity of serious talent, the editors of the big, two-volume *Norton Anthology of English Literature*, Seventh Edition (2000), perhaps the most widely used college literature textbook, have creatively revalued the canon and assigned the unimpressive Aemiliana Lanyer more pages than Thomas Hobbes, given more space to minor poet Mary Wroth than to Robert Burton, as much ink to lumpy amateur playwright Elizabeth Cary as to George Herbert, and, worst of all, paid more attention to dreary, humorless Dorothy Wordsworth than to the indisputably great Edward Lear, Lewis Carroll, and W.S. Gilbert *combined*. It's a dubious sort of affirmative action for the dead. Not content with recording and criticizing the past, some academics want to remold it closer to their heart's desire.

The more intellectually honest way to deal with the painful situation of women's absence—not complete absence, but sometimes close to it—from the cultural scene would be to regretfully accept it. It happened. We need to understand why, and move forward. Where until the 20th century were the major women poets, novelists, and essayists in—among other countries—Germany and Russia? Even as the male artists and thinkers enjoyed a fabulous burst of fertility, the women were m.i.a., which is a synonym for lost and unrecoverable.

Like that other hallmark of culture, racism, sexism has been a lose/lose formula, distorting the oppressors just as surely as it crushed and twisted the oppressed. Never mind that many, if not most of the supposed "differences" have been exposed as imaginary or artificially imposed. But culture keeps falling in love with its own creations. Recall the complacent dictum by that now forgotten member of the Forty Immortals, Edmond Jaloux (*nomen est omen)*, "Translations are like women: when they're beautiful, they're not faithful; and when they're faithful, they're not beautiful." (Is there *any* maxim starting with "Women are (always, by definition, etc.). . ." that isn't a lie? Cf. the woman-hatred throughout the Book of Proverbs, in *varium et mutabile semper femina* (and its corollary *notumque furens quid femina possit), souvent femme varie, Cosí Fan Tutte,* the seemingly positive *Das Ewig-Weiblich zieht uns hinan,* "A Woman is a Sometime Thing, "etc.)

The apodictic, pseudo-timeless declaration by M. Jaloux (d. 1949) neatly summarizes a pair of the main forms of pleasure that culture, i.e., men, has always demanded of women: physical-esthetic gratification and the pride of ownership (cf. the story of Helen of Troy). Just as revealing as Jaloux's pompous pronouncement is the casual way it refers to What Everyone Knows About Women (not much different from the knowing winks in Luther's *Wein, Weiber, und Gesang* , Don Giovanni's *"Lasciar le donne? Pazzo!"* or Oscar Hammerstein II's "There is Nothing Like a Dame"). Since the dawn of culture men have been claiming (see the figures of Ishtar in The Epic of Gilgamesh, Eve in Genesis, or Clytemnestra in *The Oresteia,*) both to have women pegged, in all their craziness *and* to be unable to figure them out (Virgil, Freud et al.)

The latter is evidently the truth, however easy it may be to figure out why they failed. Misled by ageless cultural clichés, some of them understandably appealing—sublime seductress, selfless nurturing mother, loyal sister, dutiful daughter, etc.—not least because they all made the feminine world revolve around themselves, men repeatedly found it difficult to move past their own egoistic sexual narrative. From the faceless femininity of the Venus of Willendorf to the equally featureless goddess of the hearth, Hestia/Vesta, to Courbet's *L'Origine du monde,* all genitals and breasts; from the Ognissanti Madonna to Madame de Rênal to Mother Courage, from the Cnidian Aphrodite to *The Naked Maja* to *Playboy* centerfolds; and on and on, through every fantasy and stereotype, we see the dubious male definitions of women. A collection so vast couldn't fail to make *some* contact with reality; and the myriads of men pursuing such visions and of women trying to incarnate and live up to them likewise guarantee our meeting them in the world beyond the narrow confines of "art."

That's the scary power of culture. Men indulge in elaborate, sometimes brilliant, fantasies, and then chase after them. They issue laws and decrees about the eternal nature and permanent status of women, for example, that menstruation is a kind of "impurity" from which the agent-victims must be "cleansed" (see Leviticus 15.19-24; Qur'an 2:222, etc.) They construct a giant bundle of crazed, debased, exalted, pathetic images of women—and people buy into them. But images needn't be true, only powerful. The whole business would be all too ridiculous—if it weren't also historical fact. Read the canon. Take a stroll through any major art collection; scan any fashion, bridal, or "woman's" magazine; catch the next Miss America or Miss Universe pageant (noting their various half-hearted attempts to defuse the "meat market" issue); check out the gender jokes on the greeting cards in your supermarket or pharmacy-general store. Culture happens; and much of it is crazy.

Chapter Three

The Religious Sins

¹If there arise among you a prophet, or a dreamer of dreams, and giveth thee a sign or a wonder, ²And the sign or the wonder come to pass, whereof he spake unto thee, saying, Let us go after other gods, which thou hast not known, and let us serve them; ³Thou shalt not hearken unto the words of that prophet, or that dreamer of dreams: for the LORD your God proveth you, to know whether ye love the LORD your God with all your heart and with all your soul. ⁴Ye shall walk after the LORD your God, and fear him, and keep his commandments, and obey his voice, and ye shall serve him, and cleave unto him. ⁵And that prophet, or that dreamer of dreams, shall be put to death; because he hath spoken to turn you away from the LORD your God, which brought you out of the land of Egypt, and redeemed you out of the house of bondage, to thrust thee out of the way which the LORD thy God commanded thee to walk in. So shalt thou put the evil away from the midst of thee. ⁶If thy brother, the son of thy mother, or thy son, or thy daughter, or the wife of thy bosom, or thy friend, which is as thine own soul, entice thee secretly, saying, Let us go and serve other gods, which thou hast not known, thou, nor thy fathers; ⁷Namely, of the gods of the people which are round about you, nigh unto thee, or far off from thee, from the one end of the earth even unto the other end of the earth; ⁸Thou shalt not consent unto him, nor hearken unto him; neither shall thine eye pity him, neither shalt thou spare, neither shalt thou conceal him: ⁹But thou shalt surely kill him; thine hand shall be first upon him to put him to death, and afterwards the hand of all the people. ¹⁰And thou shalt stone him with stones, that he die; because he hath sought to thrust thee away from the LORD thy God, which brought thee out of the land of Egypt, from the house of bondage. ¹¹And all Israel shall hear, and fear, and shall do no more any such wickedness as this is among you. ¹²If thou shalt hear say in one of thy cities, which the LORD thy God hath given thee to dwell there, saying, ¹³Certain men, the children of Belial, are gone out from among

you, and have withdrawn the inhabitants of their city, saying, Let us go and serve other gods, which ye have not known; [14]Then shalt thou enquire, and make search, and ask diligently; and, behold, if it be truth, and the thing certain, that such abomination is wrought among you; [15]Thou shalt surely smite the inhabitants of that city with the edge of the sword, destroying it utterly, and all that is therein, and the cattle thereof, with the edge of the sword. [16]And thou shalt gather all the spoil of it into the midst of the street thereof, and shalt burn with fire the city, and all the spoil thereof every whit, for the LORD thy God: and it shall be an heap for ever; it shall not be built again. [17]And there shall cleave nought of the cursed thing to thine hand: that the LORD may turn from the fierceness of his anger, and shew thee mercy, and have compassion upon thee, and multiply thee, as he hath sworn unto thy fathers; [18]When thou shalt hearken to the voice of the LORD thy God, to keep all his commandments which I command thee this day, to do that which is right in the eyes of the LORD thy God.

—Deuteronomy 13 (KJV)

If there's anything most conservatives and liberals can agree on, it's that *we have to respect religion.* For example, not one of the 565 senators and representatives in the indispensable *Congress at Your Fingertips* handbook lists him- or herself as an "atheist" or "agnostic." Congressman Pete Stark of California, otherwise an avowed atheist, puts "Unitarian" in his religion slot. Rep. Tammy Baldwin (the only gay person to list a partner in the "spouse" bracket) opts for "Not stated," as do a handful of other brave souls. In Washington that's about as close as people dare to get to saying "None" As a rule, conservatives either believe or pretend to believe (a typical bit of deception in *Congress at Your Fingertips* is the response of "Christian" or "Protestant" under religion, a near-meaningless term since neither denomination exists). Meanwhile, liberals are honor-bound to defend everyone's First-Amendment right to place themselves anywhere they want along the whole cockamamie theological spectrum of Judaism, Christianity and—calling Rep. Keith Ellison—Islam. It's all a matter of freedom, and freedom is what made us great in the first place, yadda-yadda-yadda.

But, of course, we do NOT have to respect religion; and that "we" refers not just to irate atheists like Christopher Hitchens or Sam Harris. No reasonable person anywhere, no calm, cool, and collected agnostic has to give the ludicrous tenets of monotheism any undeserved regard, just to avoid offending the sensibilities of people who may have sucked in their childish faith along with their mother's milk or their father's beer. Granted, voicing such criticism in any forum bound by the exquisitely sensitive norms of today's multiculturalites might be ill-advised; but in principle, so long as credulous citizens make silly public statements (e.g., "Holy, holy, holy is the LORD of hosts; the whole earth is full of his glory") about the meaning of life and reality, and so long as we have free speech, anyone is entitled to call the believers out.

At the very least one could and should try to get them to admit one basic fact: "Alas, we have zero proof for what we're saying. We have zero empirical evidence for it. Some guy (or guys—women don't do this) came down from some mountain or other claiming to have gotten up-close and personal with some invisible SPIRIT—sorry, can't tell you what that is—who told him or them this, that, and the other thing. And, for certain intellectually flimsy or non-existent reasons we *like* to believe it; so we do believe it. And, by the way, why don't you?" (Finally, a creed that levels with us—but nobody puts it that way.)

And that, in a nutshell, is the message of Judaism, Christianity, and Islam; but it won't fly. The first and most crucial reason why simply jumps, as the French say, to the eyes: it's not true. Religion provides a hopelessly inaccurate map of the world: Magically created out of chaos or nothingness, this world is said to be owned and operated by, and in sacred thrall to, an Invisible Master who takes a keen interest in our behavior, though, to judge by his often furious communiqués, he mostly disapproves of it. (365 of the Torah's 613 mitzvot are don'ts.) Despite his infinite power, "he" is strangely absent and impotent; but don't let your guard down: Sometime soon—and sooner than anybody thinks—he's going to blow the whistle (trumpet-shofar-whatever) on Planet Earth, and then proceed to the ultimate show-stopping Judgment, which will somehow reduce the trillion complex levels of (theoretically free) human behavior to a neat binary Saved-or-Damned print-out.

While waiting for this apocalyptic finale, humans are supposed to conduct themselves according to various God-given codes, which, oddly enough, embody all the ancient customs and patriarchal biases of the Prophet's tribe. Take, for example, the hair-raising punishments for idolatry in this chapter's fanatical epigraph, or the following seldom discussed, but never formally abrogated nugget of juridical wisdom from Deuteronomy 25. 11-12 "When men fight with one another, and the wife of the one draws near to rescue her husband from the hand of him who is beating him, and puts out her hand and seizes him by the private parts, then you shall cut off her hand; your eye shall have no pity" (RSV). Now why didn't WE think of that? So much for coed, tag-team wrestling.

Since the Divine Pooh-Bah who gave us such ingenious laws obstinately refuses to show up in person, his trained spokesmen (99% of them male) try to evoke his presence and keep up morale by reading and re-reading, chanting and repeating, his best-loved oracles from the ancient past. In the right sort of dramatic liturgical setting, this can prompt powerful emotions and, along with various other cultic practices, serve to bond the community of brainwashed followers together. (People who wind up leaving that community are often despised as apostates and in some cases even put to death—although scholars doubt Deuteronomy 13 was ever enforced; and it's better to be a modern Jewish *meshumad* than a Muslim *murtad*.) Its origins long since misted over in edifyingly sweet ignorance (*omne ignotum pro magnifico*, as Tacitus said), religion is amplified, glorified, and—to some feeble extent—rationalized generation after generation till it acquires not just the patina of age but a kind of untouchable grandeur and sacred inevitability. Just watch how confidently TV preachers (regular New Testament hafizes) wield their well-thumbed, leather-bound, gilt-edged copies of The Good Book. IT IS WRITTEN. (*Et alors?*)

Such changeless splendor, however, creates its own problems. As the famous Saudi theologian Muhammad ibn al Uthaymeen (1925-2001) wrote (cf. Wikipedia, "Heresy in Islam"): "There is no such thing in Islam as *bid'ah hasanah* (good innovation)." Orthodox Jews and Christians would have to concur. At most you could pretend, as John Henry Newman did in *An Essay on the Development of Christian Dogma* (1845) that, although perfect revealed truth can't change, it can, um, not exactly evolve, but *unfold*; because it takes time to figure out just what the Lord meant way back when. There can be no room for mistakes in God's super-accurate utterances, only in our fumbling interpretations of them. Just ask Galileo.

Meanwhile, more or less everything about religion is still wrong. Religion invents purpose and design where there was and is none. It conjures up a preposterously anthropomorphic male Creator. It grossly exaggerates the importance of humans (e.g., by ignoring animals, except as sacrificial offerings to the deity or dietary items for the faithful), It divides all members of the human race into adherents (good) and non-adherents (dubious-to-beyond-disgusting) of the One Magical Revelation. It imprisons the faithful in the lunatic asylum of sin, with its endless cell-like categories, blaming everyone for the archetypal crime of rebellion or disobedience or *lèse-majesté* against the Almighty, who despite his infinite vastitude is petty enough to bellow at our missteps, though not involved enough to fix them. Apparently he's also intrigued by the spectacle of our freedom (i.e., penal accountability); so he insists on letting it—forcing it—to spin itself out, much to the world's and our own misery.

Perhaps because he plays (in person anyhow) such a minimal, if not nonexistent, role in current human affairs, God and his professional echoers greatly overstress the Final Act. Christians and Muslims at least (modern Jews often display a shocking worldliness or, as Nietzsche might say, *Diesseitigkeit*) are forever downgrading "this life" as a mere prelude to What Really Matters (eternity). Other than as an entrance exam for the Wild Blue Yonder, "this life" doesn't really rate. (In fact, such *contemptus mundi* is so evidently insane that the great majority of believers ignore it, even as the great majority of Catholics practice birth-control while the popes anathematize away.)

But the doctrine has had a pervasive subconscious impact in such disparate phenomena as iconoclasm, Byzantine and otherwise, mad ascetical excesses of fasting and self-flagellation, puritanical hatred of the flesh, beauty, and the arts, the cult of martyrdom, the denigration of the physical world, etc. Monotheists also teach us that the only good idol is a smashed idol. The best Israelite kings burned pagan shrines, as did the boldest saints: Martin of Tours wrecked temples and Boniface felled Thor's oak; and the 14th century Sufi iconoclast Muhammad Sa'im al-Dahr stopped idolatry in its tracks by breaking off the Sphinx's nose. Where are the Buddhas of Bamiyan?

Although it's always tricky to assign the exact amount of blame religion deserves for the bloodiest misdeeds of religious people (who are also motivated by tribal tradition, personal history, testosterone overload, mental illness, and so forth), it's absolutely clear that religious systems are responsible for a massive and monstrous variety of concrete evil. Congenitally patriarchal itself, with a fear-inducing Father-God (we have it on the highest authority— Proverbs 1.7—that, "The fear of the LORD is the beginning of knowledge"), religion has blessed and supported the secular patriarchy in every way possible. It has promoted kingship in countless versions of throne-and-altar (millions of Muslims are still hoping to foist the Caliphate on a decadent world); it has sanctioned the male ownership of wives and daughters (see Chapter III, "The Sexist Sins"); it has worsened the habit of dividing people into "Us" and "Them."

It often seems to deliberately foster the innate human tendencies to egoism and cruelty. See the Crusades, the Inquisition, and the European conquest of the New World. See *The Decline and Fall of the Roman Empire*, passim. See the St. Bartholomew's Day massacre. See non-Nazi Catholic and Protestant collaboration in the Holocaust. See Northern Ireland. See the article, "Majority of Muslims want Islam in Politics, Poll Says," by Meris Lutz in the December 6, 2010 edition of the *Los Angeles Times* , which reports that majorities in Pakistan, Egypt, Jordan, and Nigeria approve of stoning for adultery, hand amputation for theft, and death for apostasy from Islam. Some 85% of Pakistanis, it appears, want men and women to be separated in the workplace.

In a hopeful contrast to all this, one hears ecumenically inclined monotheists constantly invoking Córdoba (as in the projected Cordoba House near the World Trade Center site). The reference, of course, is to Córdoba in the "golden age" of *convivencia* among Muslims, Jews, and Christians, around the middle to late 10th century. The problem is that any such peaceful coexistence, insofar as it's more than nostalgic fancy, looks good mostly by contrast with the reprehensible medieval alternative: unflinching Christian bigotry, exclusion, and persecution, culminating in the reign of *los reyes católicos*. It didn't correct the second-class citizenship of the *dhimmis*, nor did it abolish the oppressive *jizya* tax on unbelievers. And, most of all it didn't last. The Muslims annihilated the Jewish community of Granada in 1066; and by the time the fundamentalist Almohad dynasty controlled most of the country (1172), the Golden Age had morphed into your basic Dark Ages. What the hell, as the popes have always said, error has no rights.

The cruelties religion has impelled men (i.e., males) to commit, such as ethnic cleansing (imaginary in the Pentateuch and Joshua, perfectly real in the western conquest of the Americas, the Armenian genocide, the Holo-caust, Bosnia, etc.) might very well have happened anyway, under other guises. Apologists for religion often smugly cite the tens of millions slaugh-tered under Stalin and Mao as proof that "the atheists are worse" (though many, if not most, in the lower ranks of Stalin's blood-spattered henchmen must have been Russian Orthodox Christians). Well, homicidal fanatics undoubtedly do come in all sizes, shapes, and ideological flavors. But from Baruch Goldstein to Khalid Sheikh Mohammed, from the Albigensian Crusade to the slaughter of the Waldensians, from Muhammad's mass murder of the Banu Qurayza Jews to the 1190 massacre of Jews in York to the daily depredations of the Taliban and their Somali sidekicks, from the burning of the heretic Priscillian (385) to the burning of Joan of Arc to the burning of Michael Servetus to the burning of Giordano Bruno and beyond, righteous executions in the name of the God of mercy have been one of the monotheistic house specialties. (The main reason such horrors have gotten less frequent in modern times is the spread of religious indifference and unbelief, sometimes labeled tolerance.)

Along with the physical violence, including holy wars, persecution, e.g., of gays, circumcision, and the infinitely worse custom of clitoridectomy, comes the intellectual violence of religion: Full of oleaginous hubris, it gives its followers a fanciful but rigid guide to the world, with the inevitable result that they get lost. It teaches collective egoism, natalism, anthropocentrism, machismo, and fake history, for example, the non-existent divine highways built through the Red Sea and the Jordan River, the non-existent miracles described in the Gospels and Acts of the Apostles, or Muhammad's non-existent ride on his non-existent steed Buraq, from Mecca to Jerusalem, the Throne of God and back—monotheism has always inculcated the habit of lying for a good cause.

And then there are the non-monotheistic religions, Hinduism, Buddhism, Shintoism, and so forth, which are too vast a subject to be more than nodded at here. The politically correct approach to them is, the farther a religion's roots from the West, the more lavishly one praises it. (And philosophical religions, like Buddhism, which is more therapy than "faith," have surely made many positive contributions to the world.) But some of the same original sins of monotheistic believers keep showing up here, especially the preaching and practicing of male chauvinism. See the condition of women in Asia after millennia of religious devotion. Survey the sacred texts of Taoism or Confucianism, and note how seldom women are even mentioned, much less taken seriously. At least Muhammad, wildly sexist as he was, spoke out against female infanticide.

Rather than demonizing religion as uniquely misogynistic (which believers always deny, anyway), it makes more sense to view it as just another cultural product and hence burdened with all the baggage of the old folkways, including sexism. The problem is, religion tends to see itself as beyond culture, as *ultimate* truth and beauty and meaning and all such splendiferousness. And when religion is caught red-handed promoting indefensible ideas or behavior—such as burning witches, blessing harems, or silencing women in church—liberal religionists like to cough discreetly and mutter something like, "Oh. that's just culture"—i.e., just an ugly, accidental accretion, fly specks on the shimmering surface of the flawless divine Revelation, untouched by human hands.

Flawless, timeless divine truth? As in the old King James Bibles with the words of Jesus highlighted in red, religions are always pretending that a) there's a transcendent, "supernatural" realm beyond the grimy terrestrial sphere we mortals inhabit, and that b) certain magical formulations about this realm, passed down from age to age, both disclose and take us to it. Actually, they don't. Like every human utterance, all laws and "inspired" statements are fallible emendable, and transitory. In perhaps the worst outburst of vanity ever attributed to him, Jesus is quoted as saying that, "Heaven and earth shall pass away, but my word shall not pass away" (Mt. 24.35). That claim has to be false, except in the sense that absolutely everything goes *somewhere*, that nothing is ever completely lost, only scattered, absorbed, and transformed— but that wasn't what Jesus, or the ventriloquist "quoting" him, meant.

There are no eternal words. ("Everything has become; there are *no eternal facts*, just as there are no absolute truths. Consequently what is needed from now on is *historical philosophizing*, and with it the virtue of modesty," Nietzsche, *Human, All Too Human*, 2). The longing for them, and the punishing of those who deny or "violate" them, springs from the same sort of anxiety that fuels all protests against modernity, from Salafism to Prohibition to the Tea Party to Christian anti-feminism: give me that old-time religion, good enough for anyone unwilling or unable to stare down into the dizzying gulf of Being without any Ground.

Not surprisingly, the place where all this comes to a boil is morality. Believers, who like to personalize the world, turn their tribal legislation into a set of Divine Dictates, to be unstintingly praised, studied, and imposed. But this fanciful project begins to fall apart before the heavenly paint on it has dried. There are so many terrible or stupid laws, as Deuteronomy 13's blast against paganism shows: Worship ME! Death to idolaters! (Shariah still wants to terminate all traitors to Islam) Slavery's fine! Men rule! Punish gays! Cutoff that foreskin! Sacrifice, sacrifice! Fight the Infidels! Make Babies! Kill Animals! You're the Greatest (after ME)! For this we had to wait till the skies opened and the oracles flashed out like lightning bolts? Nowadays, as before, many men and women in the street could do far better.

But demythologizing liberals come to the rescue with their evolution-excuse: God had to take humans where he found them, and slowly move them from, say, polytheism to henotheism to monotheism, from the polygamy of Abraham to the monogamy of Rabbi Gershom, from the *herem* of Joshua to the live-and-let-live of Ruth, from the biblical demonization of gays to the ordination of Bishop Gene Robinson or (OMG) to the gay congregation Beth Chayim Chadashim in LA, and so on. But was that a gradual dawning of the Truth, or just the normal process of trial and error, of dilution of frenzied imperatives by secular experience? Did the Sacred Texts ever tell us anything we didn't know or couldn't have figured out on our own? (Not counting the preposterous stuff, like the "water of bitterness" test for wifely infidelity in Numbers 5.)

Putting it another way, what is the cash value, as William James used to say, of whatever portions of the religious law codes that may be worth saving? Setting aside the noxious or useless parts of the monotheistic Torah (a delicate operation, for on whose authority are we doing this), what about the "good stuff"? The non-theological parts of the endlessly adulated Ten Commandments, for example: Respect your parents, don't kill, don't commit adultery, don't steal, and don't bear false witness or covet your neighbor's things (which in Exodus 20.17 include the lady of the house).

For starters we'll have to ignore the many situations where ignoring the Lord's prohibitions or doing things he forbids might in fact be the better choice. (Compose your own scenario: banning the death penalty, leaving pagans alone, cheating on an unbearable spouse when divorce is out of the question, etc.) Beyond that, isn't it more or less evident that we *don't* need any prompting from on high to appreciate the pragmatic, purely human reasons for not doing what some unknown person once imagined that an invisible deity commanded his ancestors not to do?

Nature, after all, has shaped us to be sociable creatures (at least within our own clan), to cooperate and control our selfishness; and, if not always the best policy, behaving that way (or appearing to) has a lot to recommend it. As the skeptic (Hume himself) puts it in *Of a Particular Providence and a Future State* (1748):

> I deny a providence, you say, and supreme governor of the world, who guides the course of events, and punishes the vicious with infamy and disappointment, and rewards the virtuous with honour and success, in all their undertakings. But surely, I deny not the course itself of events, which lies open to every one's inquiry and examination. I acknowledge, that, in the present order of things, virtue is attended with more peace of mind than vice, and meets with a more favourable reception from the world. I am sensible, that, according to the past experience of mankind, friendship is the chief joy of human life, and moderation the only source of tranquillity and happiness. I never balance between the virtuous and the vicious course of life; but am sensible, that, to a well-disposed mind, every advantage is on the side of the former?

Of course, not everyone has a "well-disposed mind," and in the middle of the 18th century it was easier to be sanguine about human nature than it is now. But nurturing, companionable and helpful behavior must have deep genetic roots; or we all would have vanished long ago. And there's absolutely no rhyme or reason to Ivan Karamazov's (i.e., Fyodor Dostoyevsky's) axiom that you can't have virtue without (belief in) immortality. History is swarming with evidence that you can. Old Testament Jews, among others, were passionately concerned with ethics without believing in life after death. When the patriarchs in Genesis die, they're "gathered unto their people"—end of story, dead is dead. Apart from all the contradictions and absurdities in the idea of a flesh-and-blood creature living forever, it seems doubtful that the vague dream of perpetuity could ever compete with the more concrete needs and motives that drive our daily existence. When even the 100% real (if dilatory) death penalty fails to deter crime, why should some foggy fantasy of the Beyond do the trick?

Hume's good friend, Adam Smith, traces morality to our natural instincts, aided by imagination. Though we are, on the one hand, neuronally sealed up within ourselves, we continuously break out into the sphere of sympathy, not in response to some sort of divine dictate, categorical imperative or religious law, but thanks to our evolutionary past: Smith writes:

> Though our brother is upon the rack, as long as we ourselves are at our ease, our senses will never inform us of what he suffers. They never did, and never can, carry us beyond our own person, and it is by the imagination only that we can form any conception of what are his sensations. Neither can that faculty help us to this any other way, than by representing to us what would be our own, if we were in his case. It is the impressions of our own senses only, not those of

his, which our imaginations copy. By the imagination we place ourselves in his situation, we conceive ourselves enduring all the same torments, we enter as it were into his body, and become in some measure the same person with him, and thence form some idea of his sensations, and even feel something which, though weaker in degree, is not altogether unlike them. His agonies, when they are thus brought home to ourselves, when we have thus adopted and made them our own, begin at last to affect us, and we then tremble and shudder at the thought of what he feels. For as to be in pain or distress of any kind excites the most excessive sorrow, so to conceive or to imagine that we are in it, excites some degree of the same emotion, in proportion to the vivacity or dullness of the conception" (see Nicholas Philippson, *Adam Smith: An Enlightened Life*, p. 150).

So, religion is a cultural relic. (Smith was no more of a believer than Hume, just less bold to acknowledge it.) Steadily vanishing from the First World, save in benighted America, which is still grappling with evolution, if not heliocentrism, faith's great fortresses remain the ignorant, uneducated, and superstitious masses of Asia, Africa, and Latin America. Of course, it's neither polite nor politically correct to say that; and the high priests of multiculturalism will call down a sanctimonious anathema on the mockers who do. And so we have to keep a solemnly straight face when believers babble about atman, reincarnation, propitious or unpropitious days and times, supposedly real gods (Ganesha! Hanuman! Lakshmi! Durga!), witchcraft or voodoo. We have to smile appreciatively after wading through streams of theology's stupefying *ipse dixit*s about The Eternal Father, salvation history, the substitutionary atonement, or the impeccable perfection of the Qur'an. Too bad, religious belief, which vainly boasts of immortal validity, is inversely proportioned to scientific knowledge, which constantly adjusts to new facts and experiences.

Yes, one meets intelligent or semi-intelligent individuals who still hold to the faith of their fathers. But half an hour's conversation with such people usually shows that their whistling past the grave(s) of God derives from either compartmentalized thinking, nostalgia, or both. In the first case, often found among educated Hindus or Muslims, you simply wall off your mind into two independent realms, the pragmatic (ever notice how many Islamic spokesmen have studied engineering, the ultimate non-philosophical discipline?) and the theological. Needless to say, never the twain shall meet. Most Christians are likewise comfortable with the fraternal-twin worlds of nature and the supernatural, separated by a humanly impenetrable membrane (pierced repeatedly in olden times by revelations, miracles, and theophanies of every sort—but not now).

As for the potent force of religious nostalgia, it draws on the desire to linger in the womb-cradle-hearth setting from which we all get untimely ripped. Quasi-believers of this sort manage to have it both ways: They can still use the old religious vocabulary (which was metaphorical anyway), can attend services, at least on high, if not low, holy days, and can enjoy the solidarity they feel with the old religious brotherhood or sisterhood. But when asked whether they actually subscribe to all those incredible creeds, codes, and cults, they tend to shrug the question off. Whoa, they're not *literalists* or, God forbid, *fundamentalists*; (and they often put down skeptics who quote the Scriptural letter at them as hopelessly naïve). Easing into a comfortable, if not always honest, agnosticism, they say or imply, Look, there's no point in pressing this too far: You can't *prove* religious claims are false; so, what the hell, why not stick semi-earnestly to the old, well-trodden ways? As that conservative Catholic-deist Alexander Pope said, "Hope humbly then; with trembling pinions soar,/ Wait the great teacher Death, and God adore!/ What future bliss, he gives thee not to know,/ But gives that hope to be thy blessing now," *An Essay on Man* I, 91-94. And if that hope goes bust, and you never wake up, what's the harm?

Probably not much, and the harm done by loosey-goosey religionists fades to nearly nothing when compared with the brutal handiwork of hardened believers. Hence, the brightest foreseeable scenario for the future of faith might be the morphing of the latter into the former. But how good *are* the odds that large masses of humanity, hitherto prostrate in puerile worship, will come to view religion as a quaint cultural relic, immensely colorful and, at its best, thought-provoking (though way off the mark), but no more? The prospects for *that* are less than exhilarating. In the end, like the more or less sincere-but-doubting Pope, one can only hope. Merely cultural religion *would* be a relief, not to mention much less crazy than what we've got.

Chapter Four

The Urban Sins

After roaming the streets of the capital a day or two, making headway with difficulty through the human turmoil and the endless lines of vehicles, after visiting the slums of the metropolis, one realises for the first time that these Londoners have been forced to sacrifice the best qualities of their human nature, to bring to pass all the marvels of civilisation which crowd their city; that a hundred powers which slumbered within them have remained inactive, have been suppressed in order that a few might be developed more fully and multiply through union with those of others. The very turmoil of the streets has something repulsive, something against which human nature rebels. The hundreds of thousands of all classes and ranks crowding past each other, are they not all human beings with the same qualities and powers, and with the same interest in being happy? And have they not, in the end, to seek happiness in the same way, by the same means? And still they crowd by one another as though they had nothing in common, nothing to do with one another, and their only agreement is the tacit one, that each keep to his own side of the pavement, so as not to delay the opposing streams of the crowd, while it occurs to no man to honour another with so much as a glance. The brutal indifference, the un-feeling isolation of each in his private interest becomes the more repellant and offensive, the more these individuals are crowded together, within a limited space. And, however much one may be aware that this isolation of the individual, this narrow self-seeking is the fundamental principle of our society everywhere, it is nowhere so shamelessly barefaced, so self-conscious as just here in the crowding of the great city. The dissolution of mankind into monads, of which each one has a separate principle, the world of atoms, is here carried out to its utmost extreme.

—Friedrich Engels, *The Condition of the Working Class* (1845), tr. Florence Kelley Wishnewetzky

God made the country, and man made the town.

—William Cowper, *The Task*, I, 749 (1785)

Well, no, not as it stands now: God, even if he exists, *didn't* make the country. Once upon a time, one could bracket the world into the natural (miraculously fashioned by a ghostly demiurge called "God") and the artificial (everything reshaped by human—and mostly male—hands). But by now the far greater portion of what we like to call "country," (farmland, forests, parks, "nature areas," etc.) has been made over by farmers and herdsmen and hunters and trappers and miners and fishermen and lumberjacks and developers and road-builders and such. Our traces—from chemicals and feces to uprooted trees, plants, and slaughtered animals, are everywhere. Cities and civilization are synonymous. Cities, as Freud might imagine it, are the clearings in the wilderness (or jungle), the palisaded settlements that protect us from wild beasts and, more pertinently, marauding humans. In other words, they're the heart and soul of culture.

Of course, we still need agri-culture, even as that becomes ever more industrialized and less countrified. Still, the cities, where over half the world has been living since 2007, are our home base, fortress, and distinguishing feature, the showcases of humanity. And in many ways they're a mess. My point here is not so much to rehearse the familiar jeremiad against cities as cold, alienating, lonely, ugly, soulless, etc (all of which is true, and all of which could be countered with various positives, such as providing an escape from the "idiocy of rural life" and the constraints of family, clan, and village), but rather to point up some of the fallacies, illusions, and lies about cities.

The first fallacy might be the most confusing, that there are cities at all, i.e., coherent real communities, as opposed to shapeless agglomerations, too vast for any kind of unified group participation. Try that in Mexico City (22,800,000), Mumbai (21,900,000), or Shanghai (19,200,000). One can find all sorts of conflicting population figures for today's megalopolises, since defining a city's "limits" is so arbitrary. Where exactly do Tokyo, Jakarta, Seoul, or New York "begin" and "end"? The Book of Jonah claims that it took three days to walk through Nineveh; but unless a city were a circle and one always walked straight through its center, there'd be an infinite number of possible time-trajectories for ambulating through the biggest cities, and many of those routes could take a lot more than three days. The greater NY metro area is sometimes said to encompass an area of 11,000 square miles. It's like mapping an oil spill. But only a pedestrian can fully taste the massive dreariness, oppressiveness, and boredom of cities: cars and public transportation anesthetize city dwellers to much of that by whisking them as quickly as possible through the sterile, mostly treeless streets.

Such sprawling territories can be called units for taxing, electoral, and regulatory purposes; but they hardly deserve the name of cities. No inhabitant of any conurbation could know more than a fraction of all its neighborhoods, see more than a microscopic portion of its spectacles, develop more than a fleeting impression of its subcultures. What does the South Bronx know of Staten Island, and vice versa? With nearly 36,000,000 people cited as living in the Greater Tokyo Area, we seem to be talking about a large nation rather than a large town. Cities are basically geographical expressions.

As such, we know them mainly by postcard clichés of conventional sites (what the Germans neatly call *Sehenswürdigkeiten*: Red Square in horrible Moscow, Tienamen Square in horrible Beijing, Azadi [Freedom] Square in horrible Tehran—all horrible, at least, for the millions of their non-rich denizens), even as we use the shorthand of a country's capital to mean its national government. What, if anything, do the poor masses of Agra (1.8 million) make of the Taj Mahal? What idea does the London underclass have of the interior of St. Paul's Cathedral, which costs £12.50 to visit? Do the immigrants in the banlieues of Paris visit the Louvre? How often do the inhabitants of the fourteen cities in the United States named Athens (not counting New Athens, Illinois) laugh at their town's ridiculous name? Of course, if you want to visit the Parthenon (not the dilapidated ancient version, but the spiffy fixed-up model), you have to go to Centennial Park in Nashville.

Elsewhere, Djenné in Mali (a sister-city to Timbuktu) is the site of the world's largest mud-brick mosque, and what a splendid masterpiece it is. But as the New York Times reports (http://www.nytimes.com/2011/01/09/world/africa/09mali.html?partner=rss&emc=rss), the city's status as a World Heritage site means the inhabitants can't modernize their crude 19th century houses, and they bitterly resent the way the mosque has brought misery to their daily lives. "Djenné residents ... wonder aloud about the point of staying on it [the site], given the lack of tangible gains, if they are forced to live literally in mud." Like all major cultural artifacts, cities are constantly over-promoted, overpraised, and oversold. That's what chambers of commerce and tourist bureaus are for. Culture, when left to its own devices, constantly lies. (But then, how not? It's delusional.)

By now most travelers to remote or exotic cities have learned to be leery of glossy brochures. And they know, or will find out, that even glamorous destinations like London, Rome, or Rio de Janeiro, contain enormous dull, ugly oppressive, worse-than-forgettable stretches. Beyond that, the bulk of the world's urban dwellers live in dreary asphalted wastelands, or in the slums, many of them utterly hellish., of enormous cities like Karachi, São Paulo, Jakarta, Kinshasa-Brazzaville, Lagos, Dhaka, Kolkata, Manila and the truly intolerable-if-not-quite-gigantic Mogadishu (2.5 million). And then there are the crime-and-violence capitals, Baghdad, Cape Town, Harare, Caracas and, not to overlook America, St. Louis, Detroit. Flint, New Orleans, etc.. Though entering and exiting may technically be unrestricted, conditions within the world's worst cities could fairly be compared to concentration camps.

There's no measuring the pain, depression, and despair of the billions immured in these wretched places—even if the inhabitants "willingly" fled the hopeless dead end of the countryside to live there, and, if given a choice, would nonetheless remain there. In any case, media coverage of, and public discourse about, these, and probably all cities too, focuses on a thin crust of politicians and the rich and famous, ignoring the faceless proles in their tenements and shacks. The "talk of the town" passes over almost all the townspeople in silence.

Against all odds, the myth of the city prevails. Nobody finds it strange to go on talking about "holy cities"—Jerusalem, Mecca, Rome, or Varanasi, along with lesser sanctums like Medina, Allahabad, Constantinople ("the City" for Orthodox Greeks), and Salt Lake City, or at least Temple Square, for Mormons. Christians take the theme one step further by imagining Paradise itself as a city, the New Jerusalem descending from heaven. Never mind the historical gore soaked into and caked over such sites (even the New Jerusalem appears only after a divinely engineered planetary catastrophe ("and there followed hail and fire, mixed with blood, which fell on the earth, and a third of the earth was burnt up," etc. Rev. 8.7). The larger issue is the obsessive-compulsive fantasy of holiness itself: the idea that some wondrous spirit or spirits, invisible because non-existent, have come to rest permanently in a magical circle of real estate—or so various god-drunk lunatics, mostly male priests and prophets, have ordered us to believe.

From the central shrine—the Ka'ba in Mecca, Temple Mount or the Church of the Holy Sepulchre in Jerusalem, the Golden Temple in Amritsar, the Shrine of the Bab in Haifa, or the Sanctuary of Our Lady in Lourdes—waves of mysterious mana flow, that is, don't flow, outward into the brains of impassioned votaries. Upon closer inspection, the whole rigmarole of chanting, praying, kneeling pilgrims turns out to be just one more example of cultural auto-intoxication, not to say masturbatory "relish" (to cite a favorite term of St. Ignatius Loyola and Jesuit spirituality). Like screaming fans of pro soccer and other sports clubs, believers dissolve their personal identity into a golden corporate glow; which radiates from them as members of the ultimate Winning Team and thus supremely great, despite their otherwise complete personal insignificance.

God himself famously took umbrage at the ego-tripping of cities in the Tower of Babel episode: "And the LORD said: 'Look, they are one people, and they have all one language; and this is only the beginning of what they will do; nothing that they now propose to do will be impossible for them. Come, let us go down and confuse their language there, so that they may not understand one another's speech" (11:6-7, RSV). A despicable response (if not surprising from a deity who's just drowned earth in a hysterical fit of moral fury), but an accurate description of citified hubris—a culture of skyscrapers *avant la lettre*. Still, it's the city-planners, the city fathers, the visitors bureaus, the pols running for office, and the occasional writers of musicals who talk that way, not the working class drudges.

Apart from the lyrical local boosterism of ads and songs about cities ("Big D, little a, double l a s!"), note the warm, generic self-approval in words like civil, civility, civilized, urbane, politic, street-smart, and so forth; while we have a whole batch of insulting synonyms for country-dwellers: rustics, yokels, hicks, rubes, hayseeds, bumpkins, etc. Even assuming the truth of Proverbs 27.11, that, "Iron sharpens iron, and one man sharpens another" (RSV), which suggests that urbanites almost have to be cleverer than their country cousins, if only because of the larger population, there's no dodging the powerful presence of urban vanity.

It's only natural that humans should be proud of their increasingly complex achievement of creating and maintaining cities, however minuscule the contributions to it, or benefits received from it, by individual urbanites. The point, however, here as elsewhere is to keep such pride in check by noting all the lies, dissimulations, and distortions it feeds on. As it happens, the dishonest rhetorical question raised by the slimy tribune Sicinius in *Coriolanus* (3.1.198), "What is the city but the people?" exposes the core of the problem. By "people" Sicinius means the *plebs*, i.e., the urban proletariat, for whom Shakespeare never conceals his contempt, although the patricians too are nothing to boast about. "The people are the city," shout the flattered citizens; but that's no cause for celebration. Cities are made of no better building blocks than people, i.e., selfish wretches, predators and prey, rich and poor, masters and servants, etc. (see Chapter VI, "The Economic Sins").One thinks of the old northern Italian wisecrack that the classic abbreviation "S.P.Q.R." (still found all over Rome, for example, stamped on manhole covers) actually means "*Sono porci questi romani.*"

Weak as such human material is to begin with, it's prone to deteriorate further amid the poverty, overcrowding, unhealthy conditions, lowest-bidder shoddiness, and fierce competition of city life. Down through the ages the urban masses have been lavishly abused by bourgeois and aristocrats, who call them rabble; trash, scum, off-scouring, *canaille, Gesocks, Gesindel, Pöbel*, etc. And since from time to time slander and slurs prove to be semi-accurate, the so-called mobs do behave badly, as in the long history of American race (i.e., anti-black) riots, Hindu-Muslim bloodbaths, and the endless equal-opportunity assaults on Jews. Cities serve as cauldrons for heating up hatred.

Poverty engenders crime (while the economic crimes of the rich, e.g., investment bankers, are protected by law); and so the cities are full of criminals, petty and not-so-petty, most of them poor. Consider the conditions in those desperate rural slums, Indian reservations. Alas for the sentimental equation of victimhood with virtue, life among America's most victimized minority is not just dysfunctional (alcoholism, drug addiction, suicide), it's crime-ridden (see Kathy Dobie, "Tiny Little Laws: A Plague of Sexual Violence in Indian Country," *Harper's*, February, 2011).And Standing Rock Sioux reservation, which spans part of the border between North and South Dakota, though hardly a city, could stand for the mass of urban horrors both endured and carried out, by the ghettoized poor all over the world.

Of course, if conditions were improved at Standing Rock—and in the Kibera slum of Nairobi, Cité Soleil in Port-au-Prince, Orangi Town in Karachi, or Camden, NJ—crime and other abuses would more or less automatically go down. But a) this isn't going to happen any time soon (a billion of the world's humans now live in slums), and b) there are noxious elements in cities that will persist both in their current loathsome state and in any future clean-upped versions: anonymity, indifference, disjointedness, inequality. And so Exhibit A of culture turns out to be badly, if not hopelessly flawed.

Which hasn't chilled the love affair between multiculturalists and cities. Google "the city in multiculturalism" or similar phrases and you'll find a big batch of towns loudly touted as multicultural, both the usual suspects (Toronto, New York, London) and a few surprises (Jersey City, NJ, Rockdale, New South Wales). The logic is obvious: "culture" means all sorts of picturesque stuff; so the more of it, the better: quaint architecture, snazzy restaurants, a street fair or two, ethnic parades, a little foreign lingo, and a mix of people who are "proud" to be whatever. (Cf. the popular "Festa di Noantri" [Feast of Ourselves, i.e., the folk of Trastevere, as opposed to Rome's other, cruddier districts] held every July 15-30.) Real-life towns everywhere put Lake Woebegon's stalwart civic pride to shame.

And what is there to be proud of but "the culture"? The benign assumption here is that, apart from the usual taken-for-granted virtues, "culture" consists of charming, decorative elements that pose no threat to anyone (recall Balki's vague Greekness in the '80s sitcom *Perfect Strangers*).Whereas actual culture tends to come laden with narcissism, if not hubris, the variety favored, or fantasized, by today's urbanites is egalitarian, unassuming, and superficial. No room here for Brahmins of any sort, whose position makes them essentially better than others, or true-believers, who think their prophets and gurus incomparably finer than all the rest, and who thus contemn all non-believers. No room here for open practitioners of *anything* that offends western sensibilities, from FGM to honor killings to polygamy to child-, or compulsory arranged marriage, to illegal animal sacrifices to the power of parents and elders to squelch personal freedom. We don't want our cities or ethnic neighborhoods to be *that* picturesque.

So the irony of multiculturalism, or one of them, as Christopher Clausen shows in *Faded Mosaic: The Emergence of Post-Cultural America* (2002), is that even as it becomes an increasingly cherished buzzword, "culture" in a lot of its old, "thick" senses is passé, washed up, obsolete, at least in the First World. In a secular polity there are (ideally anyhow) no more sacred cows, and everything must submit to rational analysis. As mentioned, sensible people no longer believe in "holy cities"—once upon a time, *all* cities, it seems, were holy, thanks to their priestly-royal rulers and their myths of foundation by the gods—but in ones that are greener, cleaner, sunnier, and more efficiently, equitably, and pleasurably organized. No city is holy, because holiness itself is at bottom a foolish category, as a glance at the vacuous beatitude on the faces of pilgrims (of Shiites to Karbala or the shrine of Imam Reza in Mashhad , say, or Christians to Medjugorje or the Basilica of Our Lady of Guadalupe) will show.

"Sacred space" is a pretty metaphor, but it won't stand much scrutiny. When Lincoln said, "We can not dedicate—we can not consecrate—we can not hallow this ground," he spoke more truly than he, or anyone else, realized. Why should a bloodbath make a place any "holier" than other spots where humans have lived, labored, suffered, and died? Auschwitz-Birkenau is haunted; but is it holy? Calling a battlefield "holy" is ultimately just another way of trumpeting our own greatness. Notice how the main topic of Pericles' endlessly cited funeral oration was not the virtues of the dead, but the greatness of Athens and the living Athenians in the audience. Let's all give it up now for . . . *us*. Individual New Yorkers who would avoid the grosser kinds of boasting feel free to call "their" city "the capital of the world" without pausing to blush.

Consistent rationalists, on the other hand, are stuck in the secular city, which can no longer pretend to sacred status or mythic luster (nor, on the other hand, invoke paranoid visions like Sodom and Gomorrah, Augustine's Carthage, Bunyan's City of Destruction, or Axis-of-Evil capitals), and which has to be seen and judged for both its only-game-in-town possibilities (there's no salvific going back to the land, except for the well-heeled) and its grossly inadequate infrastructure and decaying or non-existent services. Yes, it's useful to listen to the lyrical, even dithyrambic arguments for cities in books like Professor Edward Glaeser's *Triumph of the City: How Our Greatest Invention Makes Us Richer, Smarter, Greener, Healthier, and Happier* (2010).

But bourgeois academics comfortably ensconced in places like Cambridge, Mass. are not well-situated to judge the day-to-day living conditions (poorer, dumber, grayer, sicker, and unhappier) of less articulate urbanites in the planet's eyesores and dumps. Glaeser is right to prefer cities to the wasteful, parasitical suburbs; but one has to wonder how high the health-and-happiness index is in Linfen, southern Shanxi province, China, whose four million-plus citizens inhabit what's often described as one of the dirtiest, most polluted (by coal) cities in the world—or in Kabwe, Zambia, Sukinda, India, Norilsk, Siberia, or another Russian city, Dzerzhinsk, aptly named after Felix Dzerzhinsky, first head of the Cheka and one of Bolshevism's hyperactive monsters, where chemical pollution prevents life expectancy from rising past 50.

Communist regimes have long been known for their outrageous indifference to the environment (the World Bank says that sixteen of the twenty most polluted cities in the world are in China cf. http://sayiamgreen.com/blog/2009/09/the-10-most-polluted-cities-in-the-world/). So there 's a certain cruel irony in the fact that, nearly two centuries after the emergence of communism, the definitive, on-tap solution to the world's ills, Engels' devastating picture of Manchester's filth and stench in 1845 could readily be duplicated in today's Third World cities, the latest victims of the Industrial Revolution. One could agree with Engels that it was all the fault of capitalism—if communism hadn't done just as badly, showing once again how naïve cultural visions of the goodness of man keep getting falsified by facts.

One of the biggest fallacies of culture is its hypertrophied sense of power and control: We can imagine gorgeous vistas called cities, and then, if we have the wherewithal, selectively enjoy them. But vistas aren't the same as actual street scenes. We can imagine we know what's wrong with cities and writes prescriptions to fix them; but, as the hapless Gaev pointed out in *The Cherry Orchard*, when all sorts of remedies are proposed for some disease, it means the disease is incurable. Cultural vanity looks to be one of those incurable diseases: the craziness is in our DNA.

Chapter Five

The Sins of Technology

"What you have told me," said my master, "upon the subject of war, does indeed discover most admirably the effects of that reason you pretend to: however, it is happy that the shame is greater than the danger; and that nature has left you utterly incapable of doing much mischief. For, your mouths lying flat with your faces, you can hardly bite each other to any purpose, unless by consent. Then as to the claws upon your feet before and behind, they are so short and tender, that one of our YAHOOS would drive a dozen of yours before him. And therefore, in recounting the numbers of those who have been killed in battle, I cannot but think you have said the thing which is not." I could not forbear shaking my head, and smiling a little at his ignorance. And being no stranger to the art of war, I gave him a description of cannons, culverins, muskets, carabines, pistols, bullets, powder, swords, bayonets, battles, sieges, retreats, attacks, undermines, countermines, bombardments, sea fights, ships sunk with a thousand men, twenty thousand killed on each side, dying groans, limbs flying in the air, smoke, noise, confusion, trampling to death under horses' feet, flight, pursuit, victory; fields strewed with carcases, left for food to dogs and wolves and birds of prey; plundering, stripping, ravishing, burning, and destroying. And to set forth the valour of my own dear countrymen, I assured him, "that I had seen them blow up a hundred enemies at once in a siege, and as many in a ship, and beheld the dead bodies drop down in pieces from the clouds, to the great diversion of the spectators."

—Swift, *Gulliver's Travels*, Part IV, Chapter 5

My Austrian-Jewish grandfather used to wonder whether all the benefits of airplanes would balance out all the evil wreaked by the bombs they dropped. Good question, and a succinct posing of a much larger, imponderable issue: how to calculate the net impact of all the technologies at work in our world?

36

Of course, one possible answer immediately comes to mind: Since humans are now perched closer than ever to the brink of self-extinction, and since we've been propelled there by the combination of our more or less constant nature and the proliferating variables of technology (itself an inevitable product of our restless evolutionary make-up), it's technological culture that's created the mess we're in. So, at the very minimum, stop boasting about it.

Too simple a formula? No doubt, but the theme of technology as both good and bad, as the modern version of Achilles' spear, killing with one end and curing with the other, is old hat. Ovid's concept of the Golden Age, for example, finds bliss in its lack of technology, which he presents as a sort of Fall from innocence:

> Not yet had the pine-tree, felled on its native mountains, descended thence into the watery plains; men knew no shores except their own. Not yet were cities begirt with steep moats, there were no trumpets of straight, no horns of curving brass, no swords or helmets. There was no need at all of armed men, for natures, secure from war's alarms, passed the years in gentle ease (I, 940100, tr. Frank Justus Miller).

And then there was cranky, unhinged Rousseau's 1750 *Discourse on the Moral Effects of the Arts and Sciences.*

Such mental flights, needless to say, are characteristic of "advanced" societies, even as dreams of nature-as-pastoral-paradise (e.g., in Montaigne's "Of Cannibals") could only appeal to sophisticated city-dwellers. If nothing else, they reveal a typical urban malaise that bothered, among others, Milton's Satan ("As one who long in populous city pent,/ Where houses thick and sewers annoy the air,/ Forth issuing on a summer's morn to breathe/ Among the pleasant villages and farms," P.L., IX, 445-448), and that we still suffer from. So, while drawing up any definitive balance sheet of technology's effects may lie beyond everyone but the Divine Bookkeeper, it might be useful to survey some areas where "advances" are comfortably familiar and constantly praised. And in a culture where "high tech" ranks close to the ultimate accolade, that won't be hard. While we can agree that some inventions, like antiseptics and painkillers are more or less entirely good, and others, like land mines and nuclear warheads are almost entirely evil, everywhere else we find a deep—and threatening—ambivalence. And so now, for convenience' sake, in alphabetical order, we have . . .

AGRICULTURE: This is the primordial technological discovery, which changed, and continues to change, everything. The most potent single force averting hunger and thus increasing population in recent centuries hasn't been medical discoveries such as the "wonder drugs," but improved methods of growing, storing (refrigeration, etc.), transporting, and distributing food. Among the many negative consequences of this agricultural revolution are the spread of animal husbandry, and therefore cruelty to animals, the slaughter of wild animal populations, destruction of their habitat, and the enslavement of stupefied, beaten-down domesticated beasts (see Chapter I, "The Primal Sin"). Long before that, the birth of agriculture in the New Stone Age promoted patriarchalism, polygyny, the equating of women with breeding stock, and all sorts of monocultures. Nowadays we have monopolistic agribusiness, fertilizer-pollution , genetically modified food, and ecocide in general (dustbowls, deforestation, desertification. etc.).

Some agricultural products range from unhealthy (whole milk, butter, sugar, animal fats) to lethal (tobacco, heroin, cocaine); and the same is true of the processed slop that the public consumes (white bread, junk food, soda . . .). Food producers are an essential arm of the addictive industries creating the surge in obesity, diabetes, vitamin deficiencies, and other civilizational maladies. Before waxing eloquent about "cuisine" (=what the elite eat), one has to consider the actual dietary habits of the masses. The garbage pumped into their brains by the media is matched by the garbage sold at the supermarket.

ARMAMENTS: When people talk about "culture, they generally mean warm-fuzzy things like the arts. They almost never think of the at least equally influential "art" of war. In 1947 the once honestly named U.S. Department of War became the Dept. of Defense, verbally shifting it from the one thing everyone execrated to something everyone had to love. The 2011 "defense" budget will run something over 700 billion dollars, or more than $2,000 for every man, woman, and child in the country—not counting all the money spent by state and local militias and police forces or the private owners of America's some 280,000,000 firearms. In the best case scenario (unbroken peace), we could speak of the Department of Waste, since ideally all armaments would never be used, apart from necessary testing, and then be thrown away. Instead, what we get is the Dept of Waste *and* Slaughter.

And while America has carried this lunacy to world-record levels, no country is free not to play the "defense" game; and if not used against foreign enemies, armaments can always be turned against internal ones, aka citizens, whence the term "democide," coined by Prof. R.J. Rummel for, among others, the 262 million 20th century victims of state-sponsored murder and genocide, far exceeding the number of those killed in conventional battle. While literature and other art forms have always complained about society's bloodlust, there seems to be no realistic picture of the past, present, or future without it. Hence, before (or while) saying anything laudatory about any culture, one has to recall its military history.

Anyone with knowledge of the old empires of Europe and Asia would hesitate before simple-mindedly endorsing any of the once Great Powers.

But, after the many bloody centuries of colonial rule, it's disheartening to see how the victims of foreign oppression are now busily creating their own new *leyenda negra*. In present-day Africa, the horrors inflicted under, say, King Leopold of Belgium in Congo, have been renewed by lunatic African despots in places like the wishfully named Democratic Republic of the Congo itself, Uganda, Angola, Ivory Coast, Somalia, and so on., where, among other technological advances, hitherto frail children have been turned into formidable murdering machines. Culture kills. It's happening even as we speak.

COMMUNICATION: Even as the modes and mass of electronic communication have expanded almost beyond reckoning, most observers agree that this is a GOOD THING. E-mail, mobile phones, instant messaging, tweeting, Facebook, and so on are just the latest wave in an incredible rising tide of contemporary verbal and visual exchange. (imagine the great lovers of history and literature sexting one another). On the other hand, Thoreau's strictures, in *Walden*, on one of the the the great initial steps in this process remain as valid: as ever: "Our inventions are wont to be pretty toys, which distract our attention from serious things. They are but improved means to an unimproved end. We are in great haste to construct a magnetic telegraph from Maine to Texas; but Maine and Texas, it may be, have nothing important to communicate." Transcendental smart-ass.

The naiveté of celebrating larger volumes of communication as a wondrous advance is patent. Since the airwaves are ideologically and aesthetically neutral (paper will bear anything, as the Russians say; and the same goes for the Internet), more communication means more propaganda, lies, b.s., gossip, idle talk, and other mis- and dis-information (e.g., SPAM come-on headings like "Party in Hawaii!" "Hear ladies scream in bed!"). Thanks to their electronic extensions, people, it seems, read less, think less, and know less. At the very least, the humble art of spelling has gone down the drain. That's kulchur for you.

And despite the Faustian *frissons* we get from technological innovations, we remain bound by the hard limits of our bodies and brains. "Yet art thou still but Faustus and a man." We can't acquire solid knowledge without time-consuming work; we don't really know something unless we know it "by heart"; we can't miraculously extend our attention span or intelligence. Studies by Robin Dunbar, professor of Evolutionary Anthropology at Oxford, show that it's impossible for humans to maintain more than around 150 serious friendships at any one time. And, as any typewriter-generation teacher can attest, increased proficiency in manipulating electronic media does nothing at all for clear thinking or cogent expression. If anything, student writing has gotten worse, and precious few of today's college kids can speak in public without embarrassing themselves. Out of the heart's abundance (or impoverishment) the mouth speaks.

MANUFACTURING: Civilization certainly supplies us with lots of stuff—if not all of us, and definitely not the poor and downtrodden, at least us well-qualified customers. The success of capitalism, of whatever sort, including Chinese capitalism, lies in its delivering the goods cheaply enough for lots of people to buy them. The market, we know, doesn't worry whether its offerings are beneficial or needed (like engineering, it asks How, not Why). And it has only marginal concerns with quality. If the mass production leads to mindless reduplication and prodigious piles of junk, so be it, as long as the demand keeps up for ugly clothes (pink parkas, say) and furniture (La-Z-Boy patio equipment), silly plastic toys, sadistic video games, humongous backyard barbecue grills, gas-gulping outboard motors, and soon-to-be discarded, unmanageable masses of paper, construction materials, etc. Once used, this metastasizing mountain of refuse finds its way to ubiquitous trash heaps, landfills, garbage dumps, and the North Pacific Subtropical Gyre (see Alan Weisman, *The World Without Us*, pp. 152-157), a nearly Africa-sized swirl of floating plastic. Culture's cup, or toilet bowl, runneth over.

But at every stage of the manufacturing process, and not just the sordid, noxious end, the dubious ways of culture are apparent. It plunders the planet for raw materials, assembles them under tedious and often oppressive conditions, designs them badly, advertises them frenetically, packages them gaudily, and then deluges the public with them. Whatever goes unused or underused or undonated gets stowed away, piled high and deep, filling closets, attics, basements, garages, self-storage units, etc. And the non-biodegradable or radioactive or otherwise hazardous waste just lives on and on. Culture makes us "greater," often in the worst way.

MINING (drilling for gas and oil, etc.): There may be a more destructive technology, pound for pound or gallon for gallon; but none immediately comes to mind. Oil spills (Exxon Valdez, BP) get the most media attention, followed by mine explosions, but even accident-free mining, whether surface or underground of coal, metals, gemstones, rare earths, chemicals, etc. is a continuous assault on earth, air, and water. Mountain-topping is only the most spectacularly visible form of mining's environmental depredation. Masochists with time on their hands can always surf through the 12,400,000 sites Google lists under "pollution from mining" with black oceans of data on deforestation, poisonous effluents, mercury emissions, coal ash, radioactivity, etc. Anyone wanting a more personal view of the issue can watch documentaries like *Harlan County* (1976), *The Devil's Miner* (2005), *Crude* (2009), or *Gasland* (2010). .

POPULATION: The flooding of the earth by streams of new humans is often mistakenly explained by the triumph of high tech medicine, especially vaccinations and antibiotics for infectious diseases; but in fact (see under

AGRICULTURE) it took a whole cluster of new technologies, most of them in sanitation and farming methods, to lower the death rates and raise the birth rates over the last two centuries. The net result, the over seven billion high-maintenance creatures now alive and kicking, will likely suffer a massive crash sometime in the next two centuries, as the various symptoms of global warming, industrial poisoning, dwindling resources, overfishing, etc. indicate. An Armageddon with such a vague date on it loses most of its terror—which in turn causes un-concern, whether complacent or defiant (see the anti-global-warming chorus, starring the late Michael Crichton, Sen. James Inhofe and various innumerate Republicans) which makes the crash still more likely.

But what everyone can see here is how the levels of humanization decimate wild animals and fashion a planet that looks more and more like us, and all of whose species exist simply to feed, serve or amuse us. It seems altogether appropriate that Christian-Islamic visions of the afterlife—when this world will have concluded its function as classroom for the moral testing of God's most beloved and indispensable creatures—envision no animals at all in the final apocalyptic scenario. Having served their humble function, they'll simply vanish. Actually, they'll vanish even without any intervention by their supposed Creator. Culture can do the job all by itself. Just ask the moa, the dodo, and the gastric-brooding frog (or the thylacine, the quagga, the Caribbean monk seal, the Baiji river dolphin . . .).

TRANSPORTATION: Welcome to Auto-World. Just as all prescription drugs have side-effects, some of them devastating, so do all technological innovations—as everybody knows. America showed the world the blessings and horrors of car-culture (Californication); and now even China and India are joining the party. All parking lots were not previously unpaved chunks of Paradise; but there's no blinking the car-caused congestion, pollution, personal isolation, pointless hypermobility, centrifugal disarticulation, giant carbon footprints, and exacerbation of the global warming that may well destroy us all.

We yammer about the hassles of life on the road, traffic deaths, gridlock, car-crash lawsuits, or the soulless hideousness of highway civilization (Route 17 in New Jersey is a personal favorite); but in the end we shrug it off and go about our business. It's a classic pattern. "Technology" comes from *technē,* art, skill, or cunning. Humans love the things *technē* produces, for example, cigarettes, liquor, crystal meth, hot rods, etc., and take the built-in dangers and evils as part of a package deal. We do this calculation (or neglect to do it) with everything from the risks of marathon running to the time and money we spend on gourmet cooking. Sometimes the facts prevail, and people realize they shouldn't continue unwise "investments" like fireproofing with asbestos, spraying mosquitoes with DDT, or painting watch dials with radium. Other times, reckless humans, most of them men, go right ahead and engage in extreme cultural behaviors like Russian roulette, Christian snake-handling, BASE jumping, and auto-erotic asphyxia. See the aptly named TV series *Jackass* and the movie spinoffs from it. Crazy, man, crazy.

Most modern cultural activities evidently take place within a broad spectrum from pretty-much-perfectly-safe (taking the train) to potentially perilous (driving a car). But the truth remains that the larger patterns of culture, like transportation, are embedded in unthinking habit and often go without the critical sand-blasting they need. Cars, for instance, along with motorcycles and trucks, have long inspired all sorts of crazed emotions (both in buyers' brains and at NASCAR events and street races) and peculiar tribal rituals (biker rallies). Americans' proverbial "love affair with the automobile" is a highly promiscuous affair, as multi-car households and individuals (Jay Lenonism) stuff their garages with everything foreign and domestic, chaste hybrids, critically endangered Hummers, off-road vehicles that cruise the wilds of suburbia, SUVs (get your Infiniti QX56 4WD, a steal at $72,000, while supplies last), muscle cars, pickups, you name it. We fetishize, glamorize, romanticize, and eroticize cars and ourselves as drivers. Been to an auto show recently? Watched any ads?

Again no surprises here: this is how culture works. We fall in love with our own artifacts (coming soon to a dealer near you, the Porsche *Pygmalion*), and use them for self-enhancement or even worship them as idols (see Isaiah 44.101-19). This is easier now than ever because only engineering nerds have any real idea how complex machines and electronic devices work. No matter, since like all technological devices, cars extend our power and intelligence; so, as surely as owning slaves enlarged the stature of their owner, the many different sorts of energy coordinated and concentrated in today's cars magnify the driver's range, reach, and control.

In a broad sense, that's what every feature of culture does: Buyers and sellers, pray-ers and voters, tourists and travelers, protesters and participants in all the arts expand and, ideally, enrich their egos through all the complex exchanges involved. Of course, such exchanges often confuse, distort, betray, and destroy—when they're not simply a waste of time, like, say, most books, movies, and TV shows. But in the world of culture the burden of proof always seems to be on the negative. The consumers of its products, like any well-primed studio audience, are ready to applaud whatever gets served up to them, be it *The Sound of Music* or the *Horst Wessel Lied*. And weaning the public away from its bad or noxious tastes is the classical thankless task: think of the countless failed attempts by Mole, Ratty, and Badger to cure Mr. Toad's insane passion for motor cars.

For motor-cars substitute any popular product of technology—plastic surgery, chainsaws, tranquilizers, snow-blowers, X-boxes, speedboats, assault rifles, text-messaging, sonar fish-finders—and similar problems, from trivial to colossal, will emerge. But in many, if not most, cases the enthusiasts will prevail. (It's a major sign of the times that "enthusiasm," which was a term of contempt in the 18th century, has become a sine qua non contemporary virtue, perhaps somewhat as the Nazis turned the adjective *fanatisch* into an all-purpose purr-word). And in the contest between an enthusiastic fan base and a handful of angry or contemptuous critics, we all know who'll win the day. Consider the success of the Indiana Jones franchise. Maybe no one ever went broke underestimating the intelligence of *any* public. That's culture for you: smart, or at least technically skilled, people making dumb products for a morbidly gullible public. Crazy.

Chapter Six

The Economic Sins

Wherefore do the wicked live, become old, yea, are mighty in power? Their seed is established in their sight with them, and their offspring before their eyes. Their houses are safe from fear, neither is the rod of God upon them. Their bull gendereth, and faileth not; their cow calveth, and casteth not her calf. They send forth their little ones like a flock, and their children dance. They take the timbrel and harp, and rejoice at the sound of the organ. They spend their days in wealth, and in a moment go down to the grave.

—Job. 21-7-13 (KJV)

Go to now, ye rich men, weep and howl for your miseries that shall come upon you. Your riches are corrupted, and your garments are motheaten. Your gold and silver is cankered; and the rust of them shall be a witness against you, and shall eat your flesh as it were fire. Ye have heaped treasure together for the last days. Behold, the hire of the labour who have reaped down your fields, which is of you kept back by fraud, crieth: and the cries of them which have reaped are entered into the ears of the Lord of sabaoth. Ye have lived in pleasure on the earth, and been wanton; ye have nourished your hearts, as in a day of slaughter. Ye have condemned and killed the just; and he doth not resist you.

—James 5.1-6 (KJV)

Economics comes from a Greek phrase meaning "law of the house"; and the first law of the house seems to be that the rich live much better than everyone else. Ever since the rise of the welfare state, "social Darwinism" has become a dirty word; but it's nonetheless true that survival of the fittest ("fit" meaning adapted to society's rat-race ecosphere) describes how economic life works.

On the other hand, people often imagine that evolution is a process of inevitable improvement and refinement, culminating , if not in perfection , a least in some sort of spectacular final result, like—what else?—*homo sapiens sapiens*.

But the distribution of wealth and resources doesn't improve over time; and, millennia after the Bible's heated assaults on the rich, they're still behaving badly. This doesn't exactly qualify as news; but it's often ignored in naive cultural kvelling by both the right and the left. Conservatives' very name proclaims their wish to keep things the way they are. Don't rock the boat; or the first-class passengers may get sea-sick. Certainly the great literary classics, from Homer to Shakespeare and Proust, by and large ignore what Heinrich Heine called the Great Soup Question. Marxists rail against the injustices of the class system, but usually fail to correct them. The biblical prophets launch crackling tirades against the rich, but that's turned out to be mostly noble hot air. It's the rare Christian pulpit whose occupant ever reminds parishioners that a camel has a better chance of slipping through the eye of a needle than a rich man has of gaining admission to the Kingdom of Heaven—whatever that is.

Simply put, culture is what culture has done; and the history of culture is, among other things, the history of pigging out at the top of the economic pile and starving at the bottom. The radically unequal distribution of buying power perforce leads to appalling differences in diet, health, lifespan, shelter, clothing, education, and every conceivable freedom and opportunity in life. As Socrates (later echoed by Benjamin Disraeli) said, the rich and poor live in two different worlds: Thus *The Republic*: IV, 419 "You ought to speak of other States in the plural number; not one of them is a city, but many cities, as they say in the game. For indeed any city, however small, is in fact divided into two, one the city of the poor, the other of the rich; these are at war with one another; and in either there are many smaller divisions, and you would be altogether beside the mark if you treated them all as a single State" (tr. B. Jowett).

And two (or more) asymmetric "states" necessarily create two (or more) different cultures. For the rich there's literacy (multiple literacies) and information, science and high art; for the poor there's functional illiteracy, and ignorance, superstition and (mostly) junk art. The rich get "quality" medical care; the poor don't. The rich travel for pleasure and take vacations; the poor don't. The rich sample all sorts of cuisines; the poor don't—they have to settle for mere food (often bad and not enough). The rich have (and dictate) fashion; the poor don't. The rich get their addictions cured in posh rehab clinics; the poor don't. The rich own mansions, and manors, and houses (sometimes with names); the poor have housing (provided they're not homeless). And so on *ad infinitum*.

But the ultimate economic sins of culture are wealth and poverty themselves. The rich rack up a monstrous environmental deficit by their over-consumption and waste. The problem can be seen writ large in the familiar figure that the US represents 5% of the world's population, but about 30% of its total consumption. If the poor countries of the world snarfed down water, oil, minerals, wood, plastics, animal products, and manufactures at the same rate we do—but stop it right there: Obviously they couldn't, because the planet would collapse first. Coddled by the plutocratic governments they put in office, the rich leave their King-Kong-size footprints everywhere: in overstocked *palazzi,* walk-in closets, garages, marinas, second homes, and stables, with gems, furs, jewelry, and massive collections of mostly unused stuff. (See "MANUFACTURING" in Chapter V "The Sins of Technology.")

The poor, whom, as Jesus pessimistically observed (Mt. 26.11) we will always have with us, make up for their powerlessness with their ever-swelling numbers. Trapped in the struggle for survival, the poor can't know about, learn about, or care about the damage they do to nature through overpopulation (aided and abetted by sexist, natalist religions), deforestation and desertification (through bad agricultural practices; see the Sahel), mistreatment and destruction of animals, and fouling of air, water, and soil. The poor do the indispensable dirty work for oil, gas, mining, lumber, and agribusiness companies, without sharing in their profits. Poverty drives people into crime—the most visible, ugly, and socially unacceptable kinds of crime; and so the poor populate the prisons. (which rehabilitate almost no one). But let's look on the bright side: prisons do create much-needed work, just as surely as terrorist operations and missile factories.

Like other aspects of culture, the economic system acquires an unmerited sacred status. Conservative ideologues hymn the virtues of the FME, though that market is hardly ever free. Politicians of all stripes (and never more than now, in a global recession) worship at the Shrine of Jobs, where the question of what Buddhism calls "right livelihood" never comes up; because whether it's a question of making Twinkies, cigarettes, Glock pistols, stupid TV spots for stupid political candidates, pornographic dreck or gas-guzzlers (Jeep Grand Sierra, anyone?) or butchering calves or building nuclear warheads, a job is a job. Come to think of it, Topf & Sons, of Erfurt must have done its part for the wartime German economy with those state-of-the-art crematoria they made for the Nazi death camps. Consumer confidence has to be kept high, because, regardless of what or how much is being consumed, consumption makes the world go round. As the talking heads on TV keep telling us, consumer spending makes up more than two-thirds of the US economy. Buy or die.

So bring on the corporation- (i.e., millionaire-) friendly tax rates, legislation, courts, and oversight agencies. The business of the world is business. Never mind that economics Noel Prize winner Herbert Simon (see Peter Singer, "What Should a Billionaire Give?—And What Should You" NYT,

Dec. 17, 2006) estimates that about 90% of "social capital" simply gets handed to the First World rich in the form of natural resources, educated, technologically savvy employees, and helpful governments (which pay for public safety, transportation, etc.). Then the recipients of this unearned treasure brag about their rugged individualism, entrepreneurial daring, far-sightedness, etc. and set up safe depots for their pelf, while hiring whatever political and legal security forces are needed to ward off the slightest threat to their continued acquisition of society's largesse.

So, among the most crucial features of culture is a set of rules designed to guarantee the tranquil ownership of wealth. As David Hume wrote in *A Treatise of Human Nature* (1749),

> [P]roperty is nothing but a stable possession, derived from the rules of justice . . .No one can doubt, that the convention for the distinction of property, and for the stability of possession, is of all circumstances the most necessary to the establishment of human society, and that after the agreement for the fixing and observing of this rule, there remains little or nothing to be done towards settling a perfect harmony and concord.

Rich or poor, everyone wants to hold on to his or her stuff. Property rights forge a community where people whose interests aren't necessarily compat-ible, (and some of whom may be busy impoverishing the others) can enjoy a pseudo-equality. And, under their aegis, like moss-covered rocks or ivy-clad ruins (but much more quickly), wealth acquires such venerability that underpaid proles who, short of winning the lottery, will never escape their congenital wretchedness often oppose soaking the rich for fear of seeing *their* incomes cut into on that blessed day when they themselves come into the big bucks. Hey, you never can tell.

Hence, culture breeds and consecrates inequalities through the incomparable human capacity to protect and pass on accumulated wealth. (Most animals can give their offspring no more than their own DNA and good nurturing.) As conservatives never tire of reminding us, radical attempts to redistribute wealth and remake existing social arrangements often go badly awry, e.g., in the hands of the Khmer Rouge or the Red Guards. Efforts to rationalize the economy always have to contend with the same selfish evolutionary imperatives at work in everything culture does. Inertia makes the world go round. And so the rich get richer, and the poor not knowing any better, increase and multiply.

One perennially popular counterblast to this iron law of inequality has been the idealization of the poor. In a moment of poetic élan Jesus said the poor were "blessed." Or at least Luke (6.20) quotes him as saying that. Mat-thew, who was often more cautious or pragmatic than Luke, amended that provocative comment to the "poor in spirit" (5.3) which sounds like a cop-out for Christian fat cats. In any event, both Marxists and liberation theologians picked up this unlikely idea by glorifying the proletariat, either as the heroic Army of the Oppressed or as a sacred people, the *anawim*, a biblical concept lyrically translated in http://www.nowheretolayhishead.org/ as "the poor seeking God for deliverance" (good luck, *anawim*, the Boss's track record isn't encouraging).

Marx may have borrowed his vision of social justice and the coming divinely programmed doom of the rich from Old Testament prophets like Amos, but the best-known modern images of the downtrodden-as-saints are probably the mechanically smiling, muscle-bound peasants and factory workers of Soviet and Maoist poster art, along with their populist kin in political ads everywhere. Today's multiculturalists chime in, hymning the intrinsic nobility of Latinos, Africans, Native Americans, Muslims, Hindus, blacks, and practically any large group of indisputably poor people. Who doesn't love 'em?

The basic problem with this is its full-throated mendaciousness. Fran Lebowitz may have put it best when she said that, "All God's children are not beautiful. Most of God's children are, in fact, barely presentable ." In other words, the poor are *not* blessed, not now and not in any far-fetched revolutionary future; which is why they're trying so hard to become un-poor, or would be trying if they had a chance. Poverty is a nest or warren of misery and vice: disease, ignorance, violence, and other kinds of dysfunctional behavior. How could it be otherwise? The classic theistic response to these horrors is "alms," which mostly means charitable crumbs tossed by Dives to Lazarus. The classic Marxist response is forced social transformation, which typically results in more of the same misery, starting out with a bloodbath and ending with a different clique in charge. The classic American response is to avoid talking about the poor altogether—because in this land of freedom and opportunity their failure to cash in might suggest there was something wrong with the country or with them—but to stress the salt-of-the-earth virtues of working class stiffs, of our Joe the plumbers (as if plumbers weren't quintessentially bourgeois,) Joe Six-Pack, pseudo-common-man Joltin' Joe DiMaggio, and other regular Joes.

At the heart of such starry-eyed visions, the secular ones at any rate, of the poor is the not-necessarily-false, but self-serving myth of human goodness and perfectibility. Consistent Christians have a built-in fraud detector for that myth—the doctrine of original sin—even as secularists have the depressing facts of history, evolutionary and otherwise. But culture won't let up on its lies: the rich are by definition glamorous, the poor are by definition *buena gente*. People who need people are the luckiest people in the world. Popularity is the sure sign of rightness. "The people have spoken," politicians and pundits unctuously declare after an election; and no one retorts that "the people" were uninformed, misled, or just plain dumb in their choice, that rule by the *demos*, insofar as it exists, is just a default arrangement, a *pis aller*, to which E.M. Forster famously awarded only two cheers.

Unfortunately (inevitably) Marx was right when he said that the material conditions of our lives shape our beliefs and convictions. Having been regimented into ignorance, the poor consume large amounts of cultural garbage: professional "wrestling," lotteries and other kinds of gambling, cock fights, horror movies, tabloids, crummy food, sugary drinks, cheap alcohol, cigarettes and other harmful drugs. But why not extend this picture and look at all the socio-economic classes as wretched caricatures (which they so often are)? In his magisterial *Laughter* (1900), Henri Bergson finds the key to comedy in "mechanical inelasticity," the all-too-common condition where humans behave like robots, instead of staying on the *qui vive* and reacting alertly to the situations that come hurtling at them. In that sense, Bergson argues, all "character" can be seen as comic because it renders humans rigid and predictable.

Which leads straight to the question of class-behavior, where by virtue of their class-character individuals frequently seem as handicapped as if they were color-blind, tone-deaf., or paraplegic. Try the following outrageous, but not necessarily erroneous, generalizations on for size: The rich are heartless, because they must realize, at least in the abstract, how wretchedly the other half lives; but , rather than do anything serious about it, they loll in their wasteful, selfish contentment. Pick up a copy of *Town and Country*, read the *Wall Street Journal*'s editorial page. Think (as briefly as possible) about Donald Trump, Silvio Berlusconi, the Koch brothers or the Walton billionaires. Google the "gap between rich and poor" (including the spoof at http://www.theonion.com/articles/gap-between-rich-and-poor-named-8th-wonder-of-the,18914/) Is it any wonder that most governments are in fact plutocracies, which transform the mere living in sin of tycoons and pols into blessedly lawful wedlock? (What God has joined together . . .)

Then there's the middle class, constantly mocked by European artists and writers, but the one class American political discourse always honors. The middle class, it seems, is forever being overtaxed (which paradoxically *doesn't* mean we should make the rich pay more, since that would prompt charges of the most heinous crime known to man, *class warfare*), along with underappreciated, and just plain forgotten. On the other hand, don't a lot of them deserve to be forgotten, with their proverbial banality, complacency, philistinism (another charge that has more of a sting in Europe), self-righteousness, phoniness, and thick-headedness. Even without the acrid animus of a Flaubert, modern bourgeoisophobes would have no trouble pointing out the intrinsic absurdity of the species: praying (or pretending to) in the pews, voting Republican, golfing religiously, watching Fox News and reality TV, cruising the Caribbean, reading *U.S. News & World Report, AAA Going Places,* or *Martha Stewart Living,* attending fantasy sports camps, NRA conventions, tennis tournaments, dinner theater, or the Rose Bowl Parade, and so forth. See D.H. Lawrence's hectoring, but not unfair portrayal in "How Beastly the Bourgeois is."

There's something essentially ridiculous about being middle-class, starting with its being located in the middle (*in medio stat mediocritas*), and hence in various ways nondescript, neither here nor there. Like the Pharisee in Luke 18.11, middle-class types seem to take and exude a particular pleasure (given their notorious lack of originality) in *not* resembling "other men" (upper class toffs or lower-class swine). And the core of this square-jawed vanity is their unawareness of it—unconscious, robotic behavior again. Where the middle-classers see themselves as "solid," a more critical eye discovers petrifaction. Their respectability looks from the outside like the nth degree of smugness. The detached observer finds their "standards" ludicrously self-referential.

One thinks of Robinson Crusoe's turgid encomium of the "middle State," which "he [Crusoe's revered father] had found by long Experience was the best State in the World, the most suited to human Happiness, not exposed to the Miseries and Hardships, the Labour and Sufferings of the mechanick Part of Mankind, and not embarrass'd with the Pride, Luxury, Ambition and Envy of the upper Part of Mankind." The middle-class is also impressed by its own numbers, which is just what renders it so alarming to its enemies and satirists. The bourgeois are everywhere. Once again, culture doesn't notice its own preposterousness, its all too prominent warts.

And so on down the social scale to the working class/underclass/proletariat/dalits, whose sins have already been mentioned. Because the condition of the poor is so undesirable, not many people, apart from bourgeois ideologues, have bothered to sentimentalize it; and so it bears a lighter burden of narcissistic mythology. But all economic classes and castes are generated by the usual human drives, greed, cruelty, ignorance, and inertia; and must be subjected to a steady critical *feu d'enfer*, not in hopes of any decisive victory, but to strive for a bare minimum of honesty.

As always, we have to ask, Is *this* the best that you could do? I.e., isn't the economy, like most of culture, a screaming embarrassment and a crying shame? And people (the newly rich, the crew at CNBC, conservatives of every stripe, professors of economics, and incumbent politicians) are *proud* of this? You betcha.

Chapter Seven

The Political Sins

And Samuel told all the words of the LORD unto the people that asked of him a king. And he said, This will be the manner of the king that shall reign over you: He will take your sons, and appoint them for himself, for his chariots, and to be his horsemen; and some shall run before his chariots. And he will appoint him captains over thousands, and captains over fifties; and will set them to ear (plow) his ground, and to reap his harvest, and to make his instruments of war, and instruments of his chariots. And he will take your daughters to be confectionaries, and to be cooks, and to be bakers. And he will take your fields, and your vineyards, and your oliveyards, even the best of them, and give them to his servants. And he will take the tenth of your seed, and of your vineyards, and give to his officers, and to his servants. And he will take your menservants, and your maidservants, and your goodliest young men, and your asses, and put them to his work. He will take the tenth of your sheep: and ye shall be his servants. And ye shall cry out in that day because of your king which ye shall have chosen you; and the LORD will not hear you in that day.

—1 Samuel 8, 10-16 (KJV)

The Hebrew Bible has a steadily negative take on politics—no wonder, since most of it was put together, if not first written down, when the Israelites/ Jews were living under foreign domination: Egyptian, Assyrian, Babylonian, Persian, or Syrian-Greek. But the problems didn't all come from the outside: Starting with Abraham, the leaders of the Chosen People are faulted in Scripture, sometimes quite acridly, for their repeated failures; and the general population, subsumed into an impossible individualized "Israel," doesn't come off any better.

To begin at the beginning, the Patriarchs (the Bible's Founding Fathers) aren't made of heroic stuff. Abraham lets Sarah treat Hagar and Ishmael abominably, and gives his wife away twice, when he gets into a tight spot. Isaac, a pallid character about whom we're told rather little, does it once. Jacob steals Esau's inheritance, with help from Rebekah (thereby founding the ancient state of Israel on skullduggery). Simeon and Levi treacherously put all the males of Shechem to the sword, and grab the women (to be raped, as surely as Dinah was). Joseph's brothers plot to murder him or, failing that, sell him into slavery, then break Jacob's heart by claiming that Joseph has been killed by a wild beast. Joseph himself is a fine fellow all around, but precisely because of that he stands out from the rest. Moses is *número uno* in Jewish tradition; but he's often portrayed as weak and ineffective (he can't even talk properly). And he gets punished for an obscure act of disobedience by being barred from the Promised Land. Some leader.

After the prophetic rulers Moses and Joshua, from the 13th to the 11th century BCE Israel is governed by the wild and crazy "judges," charismatic guerrilla chieftains who do well on the battlefield, but fail to turn the people away from idolatry and other crimes. The judges are replaced by the kings, who apart from a few bright spots (David, the early reign of Solomon, Josiah) are a bunch of miserable losers, including some downright monsters, like Menachem, Ahaz, and Manasseh. The Deuteronomical historians lump both the kings and their subjects together and betray a righteous *Schadenfreude* in recounting the annihilation of the Northern Kingdom (722 BCE) the smashing of the Southern Kingdom (586 BCE), and the fall of the monarchy altogether. Chosen-shmosen, the Israelites had it coming.

With the Babylonian Exile, Israelite self-government came to an end, except briefly, under the Maccabees, until 1948. Since biblical authors no longer had their own indigenous rulers to grouse about, they alternated between the passive obedience to pagan powers urged by Paul and the New Testament in general ("Be subject for the Lord's sake to every human institution, . . .to the emperor . . . or to the governors. . ." 1 Peter 2.13-143) and apocalyptic fantasies (Daniel, Revelation), a consoling genre that gives up on history as hopelessly evil and looks forward to a miraculous release from it through a series of electrifying cosmic wipe-outs. But the happy (for the good guys) ending remained a distant, diluted hope. The Bible's bottom line on politics would seem to be that It's a bad business, even as waiting for the Messiah seems to be a losing game.

Which sounds in many ways like a reasonable assertion: Politics, that defining cultural creation of the human race, with its subordinate artifacts such as political speech, political myths, political art and architecture, etc., leaves us little to be proud of. Without taking too literally Henry Adams' dictum that power is poison, one could easily validate it by opening any newspaper or history book. The emperors and kings of the world have covered it in blood—and, despite this, many of them are still hailed as heroes, from Alexander the

Great to Caesar to Attila (in Hungary anyway) to Genghis Khan to Napoleon to Chairman Mao. (To complete the proverbial transition from tragedy to farce we now have monarchs like the geriatric Abdullah Bin Abdulaziz of Saudi Arabia and the much-married Mswati III of Swaziland.)

And it often seems, the closer you look, the worse it gets. Take that celebrated Old Testament trio of David, Solomon, and Josiah. David sometimes behaved like a thug, as seen in his extortion from Nadab, his rape of Bathsheba and his murder of Uriah. Before he gained the throne, David practiced ethnic cleansing, slaughtering every living soul, among the Geshurites, the Girzites, and Amalekites (1 Sam.27.8-9). His last recorded action on earth was to order the assassination of Shimei and Joab. Solomon taxed and enslaved the country to support his lavish, not to say swinish, royal habits. No sooner had he died than the nation split in two. And Josiah was a bloody fanatic who "slew all the priests of the high places who were there, upon the altars" (2. Kings 23.20) If power isn't always poison, it *is* a highly addictive drug. And the ways that power has been organized, exploited, and enjoyed have often been dreadful.

As usual, political science isn't all that scientific; and we can't pass a reliable statistical judgment on the enormous spectrum of governments, past and present. Still, it does seem, not just a valid, but a yawn-inducing generalization to say that throughout history politics has caused an unspeakable amount of pain. Consider any list of emperors, pharaohs, kings, dictators, popes, etc. Is there any country on earth where a majority of the rulers have been, in any meaningful sense, good? Just look at the USA, after the first five presidents the great majority of our leaders have been useless mediocrities or worse. Electing our misrulers, rather than having them thrust upon us by the vagaries of primogeniture or some palace conspiracy or aristocratic cabal, should take some of the bite out of the miseries they inflict or allow, but that only makes the people more complicit in the whole God-awful predicament.

One could imagine that, since politics is an art, practice would make perfect, or at least that millennia of experience would lead to gradual improvements. Apparently not, since, the 20th century was by far the bloodiest and cruelest of all time, with technologically fueled democide (see Chapter VI, "The Sins of Technology," under ARMAMENTS) claiming something like 260 million victims (*not* counting battlefield casualties). Then again, Hegel told us two centuries ago that the one lesson we, i.e., people and governments, learn from history is that we *don't* learn any lessons from history (except, perhaps, how to hate our enemies and how to fight the last war).

Of course, autocrats have long been under a cloud, so that current exemplars have to adopt misleading titles like "comrade," "chairman," "president for life," "beloved leader, or "comandante." But even the most powerful autocracies share the guilt with a pit crew or cadre or *nomenklatura*, or entire party of bosses, bureaucrats; and flunkies; and in many cases they enjoy popular support, without necessarily turning into democracies. One can't even fairly put all the blame on some vile Big Brother, Franco, Lukashenko or Qaddafi, say or the recently banished Zine El Abidine Ben Ali and Hosni Mubarak, since they, like Stalin, Hitler, and Mao, have or had a lot of help. The whole orchestra stinks, and not just the soloist or the conductor.

And they're not alone. The semi-invisible apparatchiki who translate the tsars' fiats into facts can do, and have done, incalculable harm, as the wars in Vietnam and Iraq, among many others showed. But the roots of the problem lie less in defective political structures than in the nature of the human beasts who invent and service them. A glance at the poisonous condition of political culture in 2011 quickly demonstrates how far we've *not* come: plutocracies (the US, etc.), kleptocracies (Africa), and dictatorships, as far as the eye can see. The list of bad governments is a long one but even an incomplete roster would probably have to include Afghanistan (actually, all countries ending in –stan), Algeria (and pretty much all African nations), Belarus, Burundi Cambodia, China, Congo (Democratic Republic of), Cuba, Egypt, Ethiopia, Iran, Iraq, Israel, Kazakhstan, Kenya, Kyrgyzstan Laos, Lebanon, Libya, Madagascar, Mauritania, Myanmar, Mexico, Nigeria, Russia, Rwanda, Somalia, Sri Lanka, Sudan, Tajikistan, Tunisia, Uzbekistan, Vietnam, Yemen, Zimbabwe. Feel free to add your favorites.

But that's only a superficial review. One could also note the fact that all twenty-four Arab countries, while constantly assailing the sins of Israel, have, or have had, worthless governments; that communism has been a complete, and often homicidal, failure (duh); that many post-colonial regimes are a sick travesty; that corruption infects a majority of states, from Armenia to Venezuela; that government-sponsored or connived-at human rights abuses proliferate: slavery, lesser forms of servitude, torture, ethnic cleansing, police brutality, human trafficking, unjustified imprisonment, child labor, child marriage, repression of women ; censorship, and religious fanaticism; that governments of 47 Muslim and African nations do little to halt female genital mutilation; that governments worldwide persecute minorities (e.g., Kurds, Shia, Tibetans, Uighurs, Gypsies, Copts and other Christians, Baha'is , non-Muslims in Bangladesh, countless indigenous peoples, and gays). In 2009 Amnesty International noted that, "Human rights abusers enjoyed impunity for torture in at least 61 countries," that "people [were] tortured or otherwise ill-treated in at least 111 countries," that there were "unfair trials in at least 55 countries," that freedom of expression was restricted in at least 96 countries," and that "prisoners of conscience {were being] held in at least 48 countries" (http://thereport. amnesty.org/facts-and-figures).

While there's no denying that the bulk of the worst government offenses against social justice take place in the poorer countries, the First World bears a dreadful burden of responsibility for the way it has squandered its wealth and failed to aid, or actively hindered, the wretched masses of the Third World. Much of this criminal denial of help has come in the form of crazed spending on weaponry (with the US unloading more than six times the amount of cash as its closest competitor, China), a habit also indulged in by military cliques and deranged dictators elsewhere. The grand total, somewhere in the neighborhood of $1.5 trillion per annum , could be divided into two parts: the arms that actually get fired, which means death and disaster, and the arms that don't, which means idiotic profligacy. (See Chapter VI, "The Economic Sins.") But why feed the starving (1 billion or so), fight disease, build decent housing, educate children, or even (to go way out on a limb) do something for animal welfare, when you can always buy another nuclear warhead or cluster bomb?

And despite all this, narcissistic culture still hymns the greatness of nations, homelands, fatherlands, motherlands, as if they were some sort of apolitical, timeless entities. For an example of this one need only check out the latest version of the lyrics to the Russian national anthem (which has gone through many permutations over the years, keeping up with changes in the party line) in a translation supplied by the Consulate General of the Russian Federation in Montreal:

> Russia—our holy nation,
> Russia—our beloved country.
> A mighty will, great glory—
> These are yours for all time!
> *Chorus:*
>> Be glorious, our free Fatherland,
>> Age-old union of fraternal peoples,
>> Popular wisdom given by our forebears!
>> Be glorious, our country! We are proud of you!
> From the southern seas to the polar lands
> Spread our forests and fields.
> You are unique in the world, one of a kind—
> Native land protected by God!
> *Chorus*
> Wide spaces for dreams and for living
> Are opened for us by the coming years
> Our loyalty to our Fatherland gives us strength.
> Thus it was, thus it is and always will be! (Note the doxological echo)
> *Chorus*

Wow, more lies than you can shake a knout at, though probably no more than average for most auto-erotic "state hymns" (as the Russians call this deplorable rant by Sergei Mikhalkov and Gabriel El-Registan). American conservatives like to vent the same kind of bombast about *their* fabled land. Liberals (academics, etc.) find such chest-pounding laughable or worse apropos of the US, though they often give it pass when practiced by non-whites, Third-Worlders (fans of Afro-centrism, etc.) or post-colonial others. One of the world's great critical minds, Jean-Paul Sartre, loyally shilled for Maoism, though he might have learned from the Beatles to be more discerning. In New York, a bumper sticker identifying the driver/owner as "100% Boricua" seems fine, whereas one saying "100% American" raises hackles.

American women who willingly collaborate or collude with polygamy (*Big Love!*) or clitoridectomy get criticized, if not condemned, but not African women—because of their victimization and our cultural relativism. And if Islamists, following Abul Ala Maududi or whomever, want to yearn for—or fight to restore—the Caliphate (only bigger and better), why not? If Twelvers like to think the entire world will be ruled by the Twelfth Imam, sadly hidden in Rip Van Winkle Occultation since 872, who could possibly object to their deep religious-political faith? It's true that the last "mahdi," Muhammad Ahmad bin Abd Allah (1844-1885) proved to be a bust, except for some headline-grabbing slaughter in Khartoum and elsewhere, but who are westerners to object to such a powerful, popularly validated faith? When political culture runs amok as it regularly does and recently has, for example, in Darfur, one can sympathize with people who dream of a heavenly Messiah to save the day.

But no real kings for *us* anymore. Burying the myth of a sacred state with its divinely anointed king (or queen when no male is available) would seem to be healthy step forward, even if it's no automatic safeguard against political mischief. Ceremonial, constitutional monarchs only! Forget the apotheoses! (In fact, aren't all Heavenly Kings, from Yahweh to Zeus to Jupiter, just Day-Glo projections of human political figures?) The worst part about fortifying politics with religion is that it's like spiking an already drugged drink. Political righteousness, like the religious kind, boils down to self-righteousness. Hezbollah isn't the only questionable group that considers itself the Party of God.

Christians, for example, are supposed to know that, left to their own moral devices, they're helpless and worthless and deserve only condemnation. Despite that, the consciousness that they've been "saved" works wonders for their self-esteem. "Christians aren't perfect," burbles a once-widely-seen bumper sticker, "just forgiven." (Note the pleasing hint that Christians might in fact be *nearly* perfect.) And pretty soon rapture over the supreme greatness of their Redeemer turns, if not necessarily into plain arrogance, then into toasty self-esteem. "I can do all things through him who strengthens me, "says Paul in Phil. 4.13; and before long the New Testament is calling all of Jesus' followers "saints."

Parallels between Christian, or Christian-flavored culture warriors and the Wahhabis and the Taliban have been drawn many times, crusade=jihad, etc., even though Israel's obnoxious Haredim would make a fairer comparison. Even now, Jesus-loving American cattlemen are trying to breed the perfect red heifer (a single white hair spoils everything) required by Number 19.2.for ritual pollution from a corpse. Without her, the Temple of Jerusalem can't get back to business, Jesus won't return, and the Last Times won't roll. (See "red heifer" on Wikpedia or http://www.bibleprophecy.com/redheifer.htm#Temple 3) Crazy culture!

But not just in Jerusalem and Nebraska: all over the world the conflating of political commitment and holy exaltedness proceeds apace. In Venezuela Hugo Chávez & Co. foster the heroic legend of Blessed Simón Bolívar; the Iranian Basij venerate their founder, the Ayatollah Khomeini, and cults of the personality, from the Kims of North Korea to the late, great, unspeakably glorious Sapparmut Niyazov of Turkemenistan powerfully flatter the egos of adoring fans. In ahistorical America, by contrast, quasi-worship of the Founding Fathers has little real-world traction, and is mostly limited to canting politicians, who may not even know exactly who those bewigged 18th century characters were or what they said.

Still, the electrifying inspirational force of political conflict with aggressive cultural overtones keeps young men agitated in madrasas and other centers of indoctrination. In the late 1950s the author of this book attended a Jesuit prep school in Manhattan, where students used to sing a rousing anthem, entitled the "Holy Name Hymn" by the proudly reactionary cardinal of Boston, William O'Connell (1859-1944), that went like this:

O Holy Name of Majesty and Power,
O sacred Name of God's own Son.
In ev'ry joy and ev'ry weary hour,
be Thou our strength until life's war is won.

Chorus: Fierce is the fight for God and the Right;
Sweet Name of Jesus, in Thee is our might.

All o'er the earth the hearts of men are dying,
chilled by the storms of greed and strife.
All o'er the land rebellion's flag is flying,
threat'ning our altars and the Nation's life.

Ages ago, our fathers firm and loyal,
fought for the faith, forever the same.
We are their sons, our heritage is royal,
and we shall conquer in the Holy Name.

Naive, pious teenagers like us couldn't have known—and no one bothered to tell us—what all this macho apocalyptic militarism was all about ("storms of greed and strife"? "rebellion's flag"?). Some kind of leftist, secular, anti-Catholic campaign? Bring it on! A petty example, to be sure, but yet another glimpse at the ego-boosting, tub-thumping dynamics of political culture. Whatever O'Connell (a shameless egotist and power-junkie) was attacking, he typified the way ideologues cloak their will to dominance with cliché-ridden song, story, and propaganda. As always, you can't trust this stuff. We bright-eyed Jesuit *élèves* with our high SAT scores swallowed the whole nonsensical package without a murmur.

And finally, since we're on the subject of hymns, testosterone, and bullshit why not return to the Bible 1 Kings 1.38-30, about the anointing of King Solomon (part of the duel between Solomon and his elder half-brother Adonijah, which ended in Adonijah's execution)? In 1727 Handel composed his famous anthem "Zadok the Priest" for the coronation of George II, who was fated to do England and the world an unintended favor by neglecting politics and letting his royal power wither. It was, we know, a big hit and has been performed at all British coronations since then.

The text is super-repetitious, which works fine with the grand, thunderous music, but not when printed out in its naked simplicity. It's something like the distilled essence of political culture at its worst: the exaltation of a randomly chosen male as a godlike figure (Solomon was shoved onto the throne after weary old King David nodded his approval of the plot by Bathsheba, Nathan, and Zadok). Not the least absurd feature of all this is that, despite the hagiographical trimmings the Bible gives to his early career, everyone knew Solomon wound up close to being a total failure. Forty years of unchecked power, God-given or otherwise, will do that.

In Handel's biblical anthem we see combined the abject flattery, flat-out lies ("ALL the people rejoiced"?), and drunken sycophancy that have been lavished on monarchical Big Brothers everywhere, from King Nebuchadnezzar in the Book of Daniel to the countless dictators of the desperate 20th century. (Recall firmly atheistic Che Guevara swearing an oath in 1953 before a picture of his "old and mourned comrade Stalin." Mourned?!) As always, the mighty king exudes so much "greatness" that it overflows the throne room and sprinkles or soaks his kneeling subjects:

> Zadok the priest
> And Nathan the prophet
> Anointed Solomon king
> And all the people
> Rejoiced, rejoiced, rejoiced
> And all the people

Rejoiced, rejoiced, rejoiced
Rejoiced, rejoiced, rejoiced
And all the people
Rejoiced, rejoiced, rejoiced and said:
God save the king
Long live the king
God save the king
May the king live forever
Amen, amen, alleluia, alleluia, amen, amen
Amen, amen, alleluia, amen
God save the king
Long live the king
May the king live forever
Amen, amen, alleluia, alleluia, amen, amen
May the king live
May the king live
Forever, forever, forever
Alleluia, alleluia, alleluia, amen, amen
Alleluia, alleluia, amen, amen, amen
Amen, amen, alleluia, alleluia, alleluia, amen
Long live the king
God save the king
Long live the king
May the king live
May the king live
Forever, forever, forever
Amen, amen, alleluia, alleluia, amen, amen, amen, amen
Amen, amen, alleluia, amen, alleluia,
Amen, amen, amen, alleluia, alleluia

Had enough? It's true, such slavish kowtowing is mostly passé today; but it makes up a sizable chunk of our cultural heritage. (Roman Catholics couldn't help launching their own feast of Chris the King as late as 1925.) Deflecting the focus from the generally pathetic human material of kings, moderns instead worship the nation, i.e., themselves. Though nationalism in other places cam be off-putting, (imagine Burkina Faso trying to stake a claim to *our* kind of exceptionalism), it's great for folks at home: a "selfless" love that means never having to say you're sorry. So the people doffed their hats and the band played on. They're playing culture's song. Crazy stuff.

Chapter Eight

The Narcissistic Sins

O Canada!	Ô Canada!
Our home and native land!	Terre de nos aïeux,
True patriot love in all thy sons command.	Ton front est ceint de fleurons glorieux!
With glowing hearts we see thee rise,	Car ton bras sait porter l'épée,
The True North strong and free!	Il sait porter la croix!
From far and wide, O Canada,	Ton histoire est une épopée
We stand on guard for thee.	Des plus brillants exploits.
God keep our land glorious and free!	Et ta valeur, de foi trempée,
O Canada, we stand on guard for thee.	Protégera nos foyers et nos droits,
O Canada, we stand on guard for thee.	Protégera nos foyers et nos droits.

Everyone loves Canada: it's like the U.S. without the icky parts. One meets Canadian tourists in Europe discreetly displaying a maple leaf on their back packs, luggage, or jackets lest they be mistaken for odious imperial Yanks—an understandable wish. As the country that more or less invented multiculturalism (thanks, Pierre Elliot Trudeau!), Canada often strikes observers as ideally modest, understated, and sensible. But still, a nation is a nation; and the otherwise appealing Canadian national anthem (whose tune is borrowed from *The Magic Flute*—good choice, composer Callixa Lavallée!) reminds us that there's something rotten about all of them.

Anyone with a bit of high school French will notice the differences between the English and French versions of the anthem. The original French lines, by Sir Basile-Adolphe Routhier are way more . . . embarrassing:—"Your forehead wreathed with garlands"? "It (your arm) knows how to bear the cross"?—and naively chauvinistic: "Your history is an epic. Of the most brilliant exploits./ And your valor , instilled with faith,/ will protect our hearths and our rights." Egad, what happened to Canadian unself-promotion? What kind of "exploits" are we talking about here? The Candian Pacific Railway?

60

The Habs' 24 Stanley Cups? Canadians who made it big in the lower 48 (Celine Dion! Jim Carrey! Frank Gehry! Morley Safer!)? And try to sell that sword-and-cross thing to folks in the Middle East.

Like the redoubtable Canadian valor "drenched" (*trempée*) with faith, culture is sodden with narcissism. It's the nature of the beast. Individual self-centeredness is frowned on, but writ large it's accepted. Readers of "Ozymandias" smile in complacent contempt at the megalomania of Rameses II (or whomever); but this sort of Cyclopean statue, back when it was on location in all its original splendor was probably gazed at by awed Egyptians, who had their self-esteem reinforced by the feeling that Ozymandias was *their* guy and his glory reflected their own. Isn't that the message of Mt. Rushmore, Stone Mountain, and the Victoria and Albert Memorial, or the Lincoln Memorial or the monument to Mother Russia at Volgograd or the record-setting statue of Jesus at Swiebodzin, Poland (ten feet taller than the 98-foot Christ the Redeemer overlooking Rio de Janeiro)? The Big Guy is Our Guy.

It takes a race of giants to produce a giant (doesn't it?), even if that "giant" turns out to be a Mussolini, a Mao, a Mugabe, or a Kim Jong Il. The cult of the personality, which nowadays embraces such dubious characters as Fidel Castro, Muammar Qaddafi (oops), the Ayatollah Khomeini, Nursultan Nazarbayev, Alexander Lukashenko, Teodoro Obiang Nguema, lesser lights such as Sri Lanka;s Mahinda Rajapaksa or Togo's Gnassingbé Eyadéma, and everybody's favorite Bolivarian Hugo Chávez,(catch him on his dynamite TV show *Aló Presidente*) is a just another collection of the idols of the tribe.

Even as dictatorships with their leader-latria persist into our time, we see countless ludicrous examples of a tribal egotism that's at once hypersensitive and brutal. China's government throws a worldwide hissy fit over the awarding of the 2010 Nobel Peace Prize to Liu Xiaobo (how dare those Norwegian devils interfere with the sovereign, infallible People's Republic?) To this day people in Turkey can get arrested for the high crime of "insulting Turkishness." Loony Tea Partiers bristle at the slightest offense, given or hinted at, to "American exceptionalism" and slam Obama for his lukewarm devotion to it. Furious Muslims proud of having The (absolutely) Greatest Prophet and belonging to The (bar-none) Greatest Religion, see red when disrespectful kaffirs laugh at or dis Muhammad.

Culture is tribalistic, and tribes have a way of lambasting one another. More or less everyone knows what the Spanish did to the Aztecs and Incas, what white settlers did to the American Indians, what Australians did to the aborigines, etc.. Even after Wounded Knee (1890) brought an end to open war against Indians, the Bureau of Indian Affairs continued its campaign of cultural extermination, for example through the infamous Indian Industrial School in Carlisle, Pennsylvania. And the same process, in varying degrees of virulence, goes on all over the world today. Kurds are persecuted every-where, in Iraq, Turkey, Iran, etc. The Chinese harass the Tibetans, Uighurs, and Falun Gong. The Janjaweed slaughter Christians and animists in Sudan. Egyptian Muslims murder Copts. Hindus tyrannize Muslims in Kashmir and in India generally. Iranians trample down Azeris and Baha'is.

Bullets and bombs aside, cultural warfare goes on non-stop between Is-raelis and Palestinians, Catholics and Protestants in Northern Ireland, Greeks and Turks in Cyprus, Flemings and Walloons in Belgium, Spaniards vs. Basques, and Sunni vs. Shia wherever the two coexist, with the Shia generally getting the worst of it (e.g., in Saudi Arabia). Meanwhile the internal cultural conflicts are endless and countless: all the tension and hatred between and among races, castes, clans, classes, parties, factions, wings, sects, denomina-tions, and so on. Ask the "Digger" Indians. Ask the Yanomami in Brazil, the Pygmies in Congo, or the surviving victims of Mengistu Haile Mariam's Ethiopian Red Terror.

The heat generated by such tribal conflict ranges from mild (Episcopalians dispute gay ordination) to mortal (Kenyans or Iranians dispute an election). One relatively safe angle for viewing this folly is sports. Consider the de-lirious crowds greeting the news that *their* city has been chosen for the next Olympic Games (probably guaranteeing that it'll be plunged into major debt); or the mobs rioting in joy after their team has won the Super Bowl, World Series or whatever championship (preachy coaches like to say there's no "I" in "team," but there certainly is a "me" in it); or just the normal, predictable cheering, chanting, screaming, roaring, face-and-body-painting that goes on at college football and basketball games. See Chapter X, "The Ludic Sins."

And how not? All cultural expressions are self-expressions, as Hopkins pointed out in his sonnet, "As kingfishers catch fire,"

> Each mortal thing does one thing and the same:
> Deals out that being indoors each one dwells;
> Selves—goes itself; *myself* it speaks and spells,
> Crying *Whát I dó is me: for that I came.*

Naturally, the being that "selves" may be more or less "selfish" in the usual nasty sense; or it may in fact be an extraordinarily wonderful creature ex-pressing itself in works of power and goodness. But, the more we get *groups*, i.e., corporate egos, involved, with the equivalent of marching bands, patri-otic songs, uniforms, flags, and the pride, pomp, and circumstance of glorious Us, the more we confront the inborn, unapologetic narcissism of culture.

Another good site for observing this is the spectacle of group solidarity, as in the choreographed, standing applause of the old besuited politburos at the end of Party Congresses, or the *corps de ballet* of House Republicans uniting to vote against the odious, "job-killing" Obama Health Care Act: play-acting and self-promotion at its finest. Or the Organization of African Unity (beware "uniters") blinking the horrors committed by Mobutu Sese Seko, Charles Taylor, Omar al-Bashir, Robert Mugabe, or its other mass-murdering execs. Or countless Asian nations turning a united blind eye to the murderous Sinicization of Tibet, as they did for Pol Pot and do now for Than Shwe of Burma or Kim Jong Il. We-are-fa-mi-LY!

And the never-ending hypocrisy, such as the late Egyptian government's pulling its ambassador to the Vatican to protest the pope's complaints about the ongoing slaughter of Coptic Christians. Or the Vatican's continuous preaching about chastity, even as it covers up its decades-long record of pedophilia. Society, as Reinhold Niebuhr argued, is always more or less immoral; however well-behaved certain individuals may be, so we're bound to get a steady salvo of vice's phony tributes to virtue (see the Lenin or Stalin Peace Prize).

But hypocrisy becomes more appealing when graced by the veils of culture. Depending on how the word is pronounced (for example in the mouth of Newt Gingrich Tim Pawlenty, or Mitt Romney), "America" can be, not just a place-name, but a transcendent, sacred entity, so that that for some years now right-minded citizens have pinned little flags on their lapels (lest anyone mistake them for Croatians or New Zealanders) or that after WWII righteous legislators set up a committee (sometimes featuring racist or otherwise obnoxious toadstools, like segregationist Rep. John E. Rankin) to investigate "un-American affairs." Farther afield, the Arab League's very *raison d'être* is denouncing the crimes of Israel in season and out of season, the better to shift attention from the tyranny, repression, and general uselessness of its members' governments, now threatened by the sort of intifadas the A.L. used to bless, so long as it was just Palestinians who were in revolt.

If there's no, or not much, justice, peace, or honesty on your résumé, you can always plead (and, where possible, enforce) your priceless cultural values. I remember pointing out to an Iranian-American professor, who was blogging for the protestors against Ahmadinejad's fraudulent 2009 electoral victory, even while insisting on her own and the green movement's unspotted Islamic credentials, that there was some irony in a woman's acting up like this, given the brutal sexism hard-wired into the Qur'an. (I supplied numerous verses by way of evidence.) "You have insulted my culture," she declared— and slammed the door on our exchange. In some quarters today insulting another person's culture ranks with the unforgivable "blasphemy against the Holy Spirit" that the New Testament (Mk. 3.28-30) mutters darkly about.

In some cases, we can go Samuel Johnson one better, and argue that culture is the last refuge of a scoundrel. Imperialist nations—the US, the USSR,

China, etc.—often impose their language on speakers of other, inferior tongues. Erstwhile political clown Tom Tancredo was notoriously jarred by the "Third World country" atmosphere that greeted him when he visited Miami in 2006—no doubt put off by all the Cuban types and their mile-a-minute *idioma*. But, of course, he was only one of millions of proudly monolingual Americans to feel thus threatened, whence the English-only movement, which has now succeeded in making English the official language of some twenty-seven states. Elsewhere, the NY Times reported from Tbilisi on Jan. 24, 2011 that Georgia was importing English teachers (with no knowledge of Georgian) from all over to help make English and not Russian, the country's second language. One thinks of Max Weinreich's definition of a language as a dialect with an army and a navy. Culture keeps turning out to be all about power.

Along with those legions and flotillas, any major dialect brings other sorts of cultural power- structures: holy texts and sites, mythology, religion, ideology, politics, and a gaudy array of self-referential biases. Perhaps the clearest example of this is the work of missionaries. All believers, especially Christians and Muslims, know that their religion is best, and that the world is dichotomized between the enlightened (us) and the unenlightened (them, infidels, kaffirs, gentiles); so the only decent (and compassionate) thing to do is proselytize the heathens before they're sent to hell. The ecumenical movement has brought cruder versions of this mind-set into disrepute; but it persists.

And how not? If Yahweh-Allah isn't better by far than all the polytheistic competition, then why bother with "him"? And if "he" is, then everyone outside the fold has to change brands, or something bad is bound to happen. (Otherwise, why bother? Etc., etc.) Converts who buy into the new faith get a large mixed bouquet of pros and cons. New Catholics receive the casuistic lunacy of Vatican teaching on contraception, divorce, and homosexuality. New Muslims get their own heaven-sent package of misogyny, with extra perks for husbands, but about as much homophobia as the Christian version. (See Ghassan Acha's illuminating *Du Statut Inférieur de la Femme en Islam* [1989]). In both cases women can forget about becoming clergypersons. Still, the great benefit is still the ego-boosting admission into the worldwide community (the Church or the *umma*) of God's special favorites on the fast track to eternal salvation. Just check your brains at the door marked "Faith," "Mystery," or "Revelation,", and you're home free.

The unmistakable message gets them every time: "But ye are a chosen generation, a royal priesthood, an holy nation, a peculiar people, that ye should show forth the praises of him who hath called you out of darkness into his marvelous light" (1 Peter 2.9). As Mr. Rogers (an ordained minister of the Gospel) always told us, YOU ARE SPECIAL. And that means, not just Catholics, but Presbyterians, like Mr. Rogers, along with Methodists,

Lutherans, Jehovah's Witnesses, Christian Scientists, and—somewhere on the far-right, lunatic fringe of the spectrum, Mormons, plus—fling wide the gates—Ultra-Orthodox, Orthodox, Conservative, Reformed, and Reconstructionist Jews, Sunnis, Shias, Sufis, Ahmadis, Baha'is, Sikhs, you name it. And aren't more or less all of them convinced that *their* team is best, even though some of them may be willing (or obliged, for civility's sake) to make nice with others. (We'll leave aside the thorny question of whether polytheists, or even Christian Trinitarians and Catholic Mary-worshipers, might not enjoy a more-the-merrier advantage over hard-line monotheists.)

Religion, as we've seen in Chapter III, is just one of the more graphic instances of cultural narcissism. Literally more graphic than most secular institutions, thanks to the millennia it's had to gather and lay out its staggering panoply of scriptures, temples, revelations, prophets, preachers, clerics, theologians, saints, holy days, services, sacrifices, rituals, customs, prayers, chants, fasts, moral codes, masochistic flagellations, the whole shmeer. And running through even the harshest parts of this grand and glorious rigmarole (e.g., the terrors of Judgment and Hell) is the comforting message: This is all about *you*! Yes, even if it sometimes seems that Somebody Up There, the Someone in the Great Somewhere, loathes you as much as "he" likes you, isn't it flattering to be the center of divine attention? He really cares about us, "he" thinks about us all the time—in fact, it's not clear that he'd have anything else to do if it weren't for his (invisible) micro-managing of human affairs. As in Greek tragedy, the gods are comfortably placed in their plush loge seats, watching doomed humans twist and turn and, in some cases, intervening (so they say) in the action. Bravo!

But then the same pattern appears in cultural productions of every sort: the national anthems ("*Qu'un sang impur abreuve nos sillons!*") and patriotic songs ("We don't want to fight, but by jingo if we do . . ."),self-extolling alma maters, state, city, and institutional mottos ("Semper fidelis!"), the storied epics (poor America, without its *Aeneid, Chanson de Roland, Poem of the Cid, Persian Book of Kings, Lay of Igor's Campaign*, etc.—oh well, the Winning of the West will have to do). Then there are the holidays, all celebrating, in one way or another, US: from the Sabbath, when Yahweh finished the job of building the universe (or molding it out of Chaos) for his mortal friends and fans to the usual chest-pounding affairs, to July 4th (without the Revolutionary War, the US might have ended up looking like—eeuw—Canada), Bastille Day (never mind the Reign of Terror), Cinco de Mayo (and haven't Mexican governments been a splendid success ever since?), Victory Day (May 8) in Russia (no mention of Katyn or the *Guinness Book of Records* rape-totals for the Soviet Army), National Day (Oct. 1) in the People's Republic of China, where huge posters of Mao Zedong fail to say anything about the 40-plus

million people *he* sent to their deaths, or the heart-warming trifecta birthday
fêtes in North Korea for Kim Il-sung *(*Apr. 15) and Kim Jong-il (Feb. 16) and
Kim Jong-un (Jan. 8). Another Blessed Trinity!

Mother's Day and Father's Day demonstrate the wonderfulness both of
parents and the children who honor them, never mind Swift's off-the-wall
remark about the Lilliputians, "who will never allow that a child is under any
obligation to his father for begetting him, or to his mother for bringing him
into the world; which, considering the miseries of human life, was neither a
benefit in itself, nor intended so by his parents, whose thoughts in their love-
encounters were otherwise employed." Party-pooper!

Public monuments and government buildings likewise hail our collective
greatness: the Capitols, Kremlins, Houses of Parliament, Escorials, Tienan-
men Squares, the Atatürk Mausoleums, the Mount Rushmores, the Stone
Mountains, the African Renaissance Monument in Dakar, the statue of Peter
the Great in Moscow and Genghis Khan in in Tsonyin Bodlog, Mongolia, of
the Motherland in Kiev and Mother Armenia in Yerevan. And inappropri-
ately enough, the many giant statues of the Buddha scattered around Asia—
superhuman images of a man who called the self an illusion. But people wise
enough to welcome his message must have their own claim to fame as cool
customers of the truth.

And in a final touch of tender self-regard, we reserve variations on the
word "human" as something like the pinnacle of commendation. "Profoundly
human"—works of art or acts of virtue don't get much better than that. Humane societies promote kind treatment of animals (and praise themselves for
doing so) even though no species has been so relentlessly and frenetically
cruel to the beasts as ours has. The best sort of person is a humanitarian (or
phil-anthropist), even though, once again, no creature has preyed upon us as
viciously as we have. The worst sort of human behavior is called "inhumane."
See Chapter I, "The Primal Sin." (By the same token we exhaust our supply
of "bestial" epithets to describe modes of evil animals have never dreamed
of.) Somehow our ideal standard is allowed to stand for the actual perfor-
mance, though by rights such talk should qualify as damned dishonest or at
least as rhapsodically "poetic."

And, to return one last time to religion, while stressing the near-infinite
distance between God and humans, monotheism also manages to blur the
two together. First, despite its official endorsement of apophatic theology
(by rights we can only say what God *isn't*), it indulges in all sorts of anthropomorphic language about God—because it has no other. God is human, all
too human every step of the way. Psalm 8.5-6 proclaims, "Thou hast made
him [man] little less than God, and dost crown him with glory and honor.
Thou hast given him dominions over the works of thy hands; thou hast put

all things under his feet." Christianity carries this one step further by making God a flesh-and-blood human being and vice versa. Then believers get subsumed into his divine body and infused with his godliness for ever and ever and ever. Whee!

Of course, the Sufi mystic Mansur al-Hallaj was unhappily crucified in 922 for saying, "I am the truth (i.e., God)," but Allah is a very human God too—he's as sexist, violent, and insecure as any 7th century Arab male. Ignoring this, many other Muslim mystics have looked past Allah's downsides and enjoyed surrendering to and dissolving into the divine essence, whatever that is. God, like all cultural creations, is all about us. Smeared all over as "he" is with our fingerprints, he reminds us of ourselves; he makes us look good and feel good. Yes, theists know how far beneath their God they rank, just as sports fans admit to being infinitely less skilled than the baseball, football, basketball, hockey, etc. professionals they cheer for (see Chapter X, "The Ludic Sins"). Fans can't actually compete, but they can wear the numbered and named jerseys; and their merely noisy or blissed-out presence constitutes the always formidable home-field advantage. Greatness is infectious.

Narcissus may have been the first artist (post-creation). By staring into the pond he fashioned a beautiful, if insubstantial, image. Being human, he fell in love with it—to the point of death, as humans sometimes do. Meantime, he failed to notice both the absurdity of the whole process and the severely limited nature of the artist-hero, himself. And largely forgotten in the story is the female victim, Echo, who wasted away and died of neglect. So, it's a perfect symbol of crazy culture.

Chapter Nine

The Artistic Sins

In eldest time, e'er mortals writ or read,
E'er Pallas issued from the Thunderer's head,
Dulness o'er all possessed her ancient right,
Daughter of Chaos and eternal Night:
Fate in their dotage this fair idiot gave,
Gross as her sire, and as her mother grave,
Laborious, heavy, busy, bold, and blind,
She ruled in native anarchy, the mind.
Still her old empire to restore she tries,
For, born a goddess, Dulness never dies.

—Alexander Pope, *The Dunciad* I, 9-18

The arts, it goes without saying, are the crowning glory of civilization, whence all the museums, libraries, cinemas, theaters, concert halls, Barnes & Nobles, Borders (whoa, bankruptcy court), Oscars Emmys, TONYs, Nobels, Bookers, and other awards, etc. Even clueless America honors its creative minds in a myriad ways and teaches their work to its youth. The problem here is a seriously warped perspective: when people talk about "artists" and "artistic heritage," they refer, not to the total body of performances and the written or recorded or otherwise quasi-permanent versions of them, but to the top of the line, the classics in the field, the stuff widely accepted as best. Meanwhile, the overwhelming majority of *objets d'art* has always been, and is now more than ever, mediocre, slapdash, undistinguished, not to say crap.

How to quantify and qualify all this material? Obviously no individual or group could evaluate the total artistic production of any given year from any given (populous) culture, much less the whole damn planet's. But before trying to document, however impressionistically, the third-ratedness of all the arts, one might well start off with a sensible a priori: Since the creative (and intellectual and imaginative) gifts of most professional artists—not to mention the ever-growing body of pretend-artists and frauds—are, extremely limited, how could the bulk of their "achievements" *not* range from so-so to poor to piddling? How could the warehouses full of books, periodicals, TV tapes, DVDs, CDs, photos, fashion designs, etc. *not* be bursting with bilge?

You know, whodunits, tell-alls, how-to-do-it manuals, bodice-rippers, airport lit, self-help and inspirational bios, fashion magazines, rap albums, porn DVDs, video games, and the whole dreary spectrum of popular culture from Hannah Montana to Thomas Kincaid-forgotten as soon it's consumed. The furnishers of these materials remind one of what Plato said about the hoi polloi, who digest such confections: "My dear Crito, I only wish the many could do the greatest mischief, so that they could also do the greatest good! That would be well indeed. As it is, they can do neither; for they cannot make a man either wise or foolish; they do things quite at random" (Crito 43C, tr. W.H.D. Rouse).

And now for a first quick sample of the pop parade:

Top Tunes singles and albums, Dec. 21, 2010, Associated Press:

Singles:

1. "Grenade," Bruno Mars
2. "Firework," Katy Perry
3. "6 Foot 7 Foot (feat. Cory Gunz)," Lil Wayne, Cory Gunz
4. "The Time (Dirty Bit)," Black Eyed Peas
5. "What's My Name?" Rihanna, Drake
6. "We R Who We R," Ke$ha
7. "Raise Your Glass," P!nk
8. "Black and Yellow," Wiz Khalifa
9. "Tonight (feat. Ludacris & DJ Frank E)," Enrique Iglesias
10. "Bottoms Up (feat. Nicki Minaj)," Trey Songz

Albums:

1. "TRON: Legacy," Daft Punk
2. "Glee: The Music—The Christmas Album," Glee Cast
3. "Love Letter," R. Kelly
4. "Michael," *Michael* Jackson
5. My Beautiful Dark Twisted Fantasy," Kanye West
6. "Last Train to Paris," Diddy—Dirty Money
7. "Sigh No More," Mumford & Sons

8. "Doo-Wops & Hooligans," Bruno Mars
9. "Farmer's Daughter," Crystal Bowersox
10. "No Mercy," T.I.

Whew. Mediocrity (and worse) rules. For the more or less definitive evidence of this, one need only scan the usual registers of cultural popularity: the bestseller lists, the top 40 charts, the offerings at your local Cineplex, the end-of-the-year roundups. Sampling their contents can lead to a number of (non-) remarkable discoveries, such as the persistence of superheroes (male) with preternatural powers, the proliferation of scenarios for Armageddon, the enormous role played by vampires, zombies, and aliens in public and private life, the virtual non-existence of sexually transmitted diseases, and, of course, fodder for the in-depth analysis of artistic behavior known as celebritology. Americans, like other humans, aren't hypocrites in their pleasures; so what they buy proclaims their feeble judgment and abominable taste. This has no doubt always been true, though for the last few centuries it's been exacerbated by the mass production and marketing of art (junk food for the mind).

But that's not how we habitually talk about the arts. By the fuzzy math of synecdoche we equate the tiny percentage of towering masterpieces with the inglorious whole. (In a similar sleight of hand we substitute a familiar architectural icon, e.g., the Gateway Arch of St. Louis or the Sydney Opera House, for the unremarkable towns they're planted in, see Chapter IV, "The Urban Sins.") And in an even more laughable distortion, members of a particular culture often like to associate themselves with its great past geniuses, as if they could somehow claim credit for being a member of the same club. Thus the portraits of great or near-great creative figures (Debussy, Saint-Exupéry, Cezanne, Eiffel, the Curies) that used to adorn French banknotes, or, to reduce unearned cultural pride to the absurd, Sarah Palin's defense of her malapropism "refudiate": "English is a living language. . . Shakespeare liked to coin new words. Got to celebrate it!" Even so (see Chapter X, "The Ludic Sins") fat, out-of-breath, middle-aged males, who couldn't run the length of the gridiron without a seizure, plunk down on couches cheering players whose prowess, they imagine, makes *them* look good by electronic osmosis.

Of course, we'd have a paradoxically different problem if, *per impossibile*, the everyday cultural landscape were piled high with works of genius: we could barely scratch the surface of it all; and our chief aesthetic experience would be bitter frustration, a hundred times worse than Greekless Petrarch's sighing over his unread manuscript of Homer. But that's an idle thought; (and in any case there's still enough splendid stuff to keep anyone busy for lifetimes). The larger truth is that works that last, works that demand revisiting (*einmal ist keinmal*, as the Germans say), books that meet Kafka's criterion of being an ice axe to break the frozen sea inside us are the dramatic exception that proves the depressing rule.

But who could ever fully catalogue the massive, steaming piles of *dreck* that issue from the world's culture mills? As Pope makes Homer say, "To count them all, demands a thousand Tongues,/A Throat of Brass, and Adamantine Lungs" (*Iliad*, II, 580-581). Failing that, here's a random list of general and particular cultural garbage, familiar to most observers of the American scene, though by no means limited to the vast marketplace of mediocrity-or-worse that stretches from sea to shining sea:

ads (the most common form of public "speech," scientifically adjusted to the audience's Lowest Common Denominator; in its higher manifestations the lowest form of art—except when the ads are more skillful or amusing than the snore-worthy pages or chunks of air-time they're paying for).

American beer (the blandest brands brewed less to be drunk than to be trucked and distributed, even as processed foods are designed primarily to be shipped and sold, not eaten).

American Idol, Dancing with the Stars, and other similar "talent" shows (archetypal egalitarian entertainment: hey, we're ALL talented, sort of, and who better to judge talent than us idolizers?)

"Associates" (laughable neologism for serfs toiling at Wal-Mart and other big-box stores, as if they were part of the corporation's inner core, like associate professor, associate dean, associate partner, etc. See related euphemisms such as correctional facility, developmentally challenged, administrative assistant, etc.).

boxing (the fine "art" of mashing and maiming, endlessly romanticized by Hollywood, which never met a boxer it didn't like; see *Somebody Up There Likes Me, Rocky I-V, Ali, Million Dollar Baby, The Fighter*, etc.).

chick-lit (throwaway genre establishing women's inalienable right to be as banal and stupid as men).

country music (practically all of it, a giant, plastic box of formulated twangs and by-the-numbers heartbreak, with pseudo-rusticity mirroring its pseudo-authenticity).

fast food (the *basse cuisine* that conquered the world: egalitarian dining: anybody can cook it, anybody can buy it, anybody can eat it). Latest stats indicate 31,000 McDonald's "restaurants" worldwide in 119 (or maybe 122) countries, serving 58,000,000 customers a day. If that's not progress, what is?

game shows (an informational democracy, where "trivia" is a sacred institution and plutocratic networks spread the wealth).

horror films (now in steep decline, once rich grazing land for misfits, jerks, and creeps).

Halloween (America's leading secular holiday and a major cultural festival celebrating . . .what? stale macabre jokes, fake *frissons*, moronic costumes, irritating, candy-gorging juvenile mendicants).

Las Vegas (either sanitized or raunchy versions, Heaven-on-Earth for the brain-dead; note the incorporation of major cultural icons in New York-, Paris-, Venice-, ancient Rome- and Egypt-themed hotels).

McMansions (a victim of the Great Recession and common sense, enough remain to recall a bygone era of stupidity, insecurity, and pretentiousness).

nightly news (late-breaking, muck-raking , headline-making pre-digested pulp for uninformed folk-in-a-hurry).

poetry slams (yet another kind of democratized quasi-art in contest-form to make it more, like, um, you know what I'm sayin', *relevant*).

pornography (*the* most important art form of our time, ranging from the amusingly clumsy to the utterly disgusting; even Sartre admitted that it *does* make the time pass).

rap (*le dernier cri* of music, in more ways than one; unites the highest testosterone content with the lowest melodic content).

Real Housewives shows (semi-scripted auto-degradation, one of a vast assortment of TV genres designed to make dullish viewers feel smarter than the beyond-stupid protagonists. Is this what people mean by "post-feminism"? As in all reality TV ["reality" being whatever the networks and Hollywood say it is], the staple fare is inarticulate morons sounding off on the two most vital topics of American youth, "personalities" and "relationships." The actual "events" in the "lives" of the protagonists then become part of the cable news cycle).

romance novels (75 million Americans read at least one a year, fake-lit composed by robots for robots).

Saturday morning cartoons (introductory brain rot for rug-rats, minimalist baby-sitting; badly drawn, stupidly scripted, clumsily voiced, a fitting preparation for the lifetime drivel of "adult" programming).

Sit-coms (mostly soap operas [see below] with laugh tracks; forgettable fluff, if at times faintly subversive, e.g., the recurrent trope of the all-wise wife and the inept, oafish husband; in a wink at feminism, women are depicted as knowing what's best, despite their powerlessness, which they accept with ironic grace).

Soap operas (not the giant icons they used to be, but a useful indicator of the lame, formulaic, melodramatic stories popular culture tells. Compare with the more elaborately produced but consistently worthless fare served up by video stores, Netflix, Movies on Demand, etc.).

Supermarket tabloids ("news" for semi-literate anthropoidal apes; tapping into the rich Hey, Who Can Say? vein of American culture, rags like *The National Enquirer* expand the frontiers of knowledge with stories unobtainable elsewhere, " Heaven Photographed by Hubble Telescope," "Two-Headed Space Alien Shot by Farmer," "FBI Captures Bat Child," "Fat Tourist Wrecks Tower of Pisa," etc.).

Tattoos (cf. the NBA and pro sports in general: athletes now deface their sexily muscled skin with dumb graffiti; beyond that, untold millions of males and females proudly flash their prison-themed, Chinese character, Maori-or-whatever designs. Overwhelmingly trite or silly [stars, flags, flowers, eagles, angels, etc.], tattoos are highly popular with porn stars, some of whom, in a classic trope of cognitive dissonance, also like to wear crosses on their ears or around their necks whilst fornicating. See the documentary *Alix Lambert's Mark of Cain*).

Theme parks (Disney World! Knott's Berry Farm! SeaWorld! Six Flags [all 21 throughout North America]! Busch Gardens! The Wizarding World of Harry Potter!): world's largest playpens.

Video games (the supreme post-toddlerhood toy of modern times; though often flabby and unfit, socially deficient and colorless, gamers register staggering body counts and wreak electronic mayhem, which does little to prepare them for their future careers as fighter pilots or terrorists).

And then there are the Cultural Stars, the countless "personalities" officially certified as famous-for-being-well-known. Like the ephemeral offal they deliver to the public, some of it just worthless (see the "Top Tunes" cited earlier), some of it truly rotten (see any collection of commercial greeting cards or all items in "Bargain Books" sales), these "celebrities" will soon be buried in oblivion, but only to be replaced by similar lime-lit nonentities. Granted, they're often worse—esthetically, intellectually, morally or otherwise—than average; but their fame (ca. 2010) reminds us that the public, when so inclined, will buy almost any trash in bulk. Culture is now a supermarket, and the sight of the overflowing shopping carts that people push through the check-out aisles into the parking lot is enough to make any thoughtful person cringe: the literary, musical, political, philosophical, etc, equivalent of products like Cocoa Puffs, Dr. Pepper, Lunchables, Red Bull, margarine, hot dogs, microwave popcorn or Cheez Whiz. Hey, it's a free country.

Well, in a way it is, however predetermined the dietary and cultural tastes of the consumer may be. Nobody's forcing purchasers to vote with their wallets or leisure time for the tawdry-grubby stuff they prefer. But, once again, why pretend that "culture" is some ideal Platonic realm of rarefied perfection? The arts are the sum total of what "artists" (Hollywood's favorite self-descriptor) actually dish up and their audience actually knocks down. And now that this enormous glut of material is available for inspection on the Web, no unbiased judge could deny the fact that, as young Americans are likely to say about almost anything these days, the bulk of our songs, shows, stories, movies, pictures, books, albums, buildings, and public speech of every sort, quite simply, *sucks.* And, one might add, sucks out what's left of people's brains.

At times one may be torn between pinning most of the blame on either the cynical suppliers and sellers of cultural junk or the low-wattage buyers of it; but it's a heavy-breathing collaboration. And the undeniable reality of the titanic market share commanded by such stercoraceous material inflicts a massive, if not quite fatal, wound on the very term and concept (the *Begriff,* as the Germans say) of culture. Any attempt to dim the lights, bow one's head, and play or listen to organ music when the word "culture" is uttered can only be laughed to scorn.

Chapter Ten

The Ludic Sins

The association between human sacrifice and the ballgame appears rather late in the archaeological record, no earlier than the Classic era. The association was particularly strong within the Classic Veracruz and the Maya cultures, where the most explicit depictions of human sacrifice can be seen on the ballcourt panels — for example at El Tajin (850-1100 CE)ⁱ and at Chichen Itza (900-1200 CE) — as well as on the well-known decapitated ballplayer stelae from the Classic Veracruz site of Aparicio (700-900 CE). The Postclassic Maya religious and quasi-historical narrative, the *Popul Vuh* also links human sacrifice with the ballgame . . .. Captives were often shown in Maya art, and it is assumed that these captives were sacrificed after losing a rigged ritual ballgame. Rather than nearly nude and sometimes battered captives, however, the ballcourts at El Tajin and Chichen Itza show the sacrifice of practiced ballplayers, perhaps the captain of a team. Decapitation is particularly associated with the ballgame—severed heads are featured in much Late Classic ballgame art and appear repeatedly in the *Popol Vul.* With the Aztec version of the game, the skulls of losing team members were even placed in a 'skull rack' besides the field, and their blood was offered as 'food for the gods.' There has even been speculation that the heads and skulls were used as balls.

—From the Wikipedia article, "Mesoamerican ballgame"

Nothing culture does is innocent; and so even the world of sport can't shed "the human stain." Once amateur play, sports are now mostly professional or pre-professional entertainment; and while games no longer end with human sacrifice (apart from the occasional coach being fired), the violent core remains the same. Auto racers crash, boxers, practitioners of the "sweet science," batter each other's brains, bodies, and faces, ditto for mixed martial "artists" football players stagger (or get carried on stretchers) off the field with concussions, jockeys ride thoroughbreds to death, hockey players box, wrestle, and rearrange teeth without an orthodontist's license, baseball players have bench-clearing brawls, and basketball players hack, whack, and attack whoever has the ball. And the crowds cheer away.

Well, everyone knows about that; and, besides, the worst perpetrators, most of them, *do* get punished and fined, even if that only amounts to the tiniest dent in their enormous salaries. But one needs to review and reject, or at least rein in, the standard clichés of sports culture. First and worst, that the whole business is a Very Big Deal. Consider the global frenzy of the World Cup or the Olympics, with the flag-waving, national anthems, and tribal eruptions, and where just deciding on the venue is a five-act political farce, larded with bribes and unseemly shenanigans.

And then there's the behavior of the rightly named fan(atic)s, from WWF yahoos to British soccer goons to free-swinging fathers of Little Leaguers (Pop Warner, peewee hockey, etc. players,) and to the screaming crowds in the stands at contests all over the planet. A culture of wretched excess surrounds games with hoopla before and optional donnybrooks afterwards, with cheerleaders, mascots, marching bands, team chants, colors, caps, and bumper stickers, with vuvuzelas, sound-and-light effects (whenever the home team scores),prizes and parades, vociferous announcers, play-by-play callers, color commentators, sports magazines, TV shows, and "personalities," and the inevitable extras: booze, betting, and steroids. Ain't we got fun.

Much has always been made, and rightly, of sport's therapeutic contribution to life, and of all the virtues and values it "builds." Teamwork, fair play (even though in strict orthodoxy winning is still the only thing), *mens sana in corpore sano*, why not? But even if we grant all that (to amateur athletics, at least), the negatives have to be noted, especially in sports where muscular collisions are always bordering on, if not degenerating into, open violence. Sports terms are revealing: teams beat, blast, crush, bury, or rout one another. If they don't get edged, losers may find themselves slaughtered, walloped, drubbed or wiped out. "We will—we will—ROCK you!" "Hit 'em again, hit 'em again, harder, HARDER!"

It's no accident that men's sports are more lively and exciting than the women's versions: Athletics borrow from, and are a show window for, the combative skills that evolution long selected for—speed in chasing prey or enemies, strength in fighting and laying them low, agility in maneuvering, with as much controlled ferocity as possible. So, women don't compete against men (with the minor exception of mixed doubles in tennis), and women play softball instead of hardball, don't body-check in hockey, don't play tackle football at all, and use a smaller basketball. (Then again there's always roller derby.) Sport in general is still more a man's than a woman's world and likely to remain so. It's no accident that we call athletes jocks—and notice the irony that the contents of a jock strap shrink after a steroid regimen. Some kinds of manliness have to be sacrificed to a higher goal.

Another obvious indicator of the high testosterone content of sports is the emotional eruptions it causes: from the proverbial' "thrill of victory" and "agony of defeat" (whatever happened to the serenity of draws?) for participants to the fans' exultation and depression, rage over players' and managers' errors and refs' blown calls, and all the usual routines of male sentimentality. How not laugh to see the way feeble, flabby, out-of-shape, aging men identify with their godlike jock heroes (variations on SNL's "Duh Bears!" crew). Field of Dream indeed. The boys and their toys.

So, it appears that professional team-sports, everywhere in the world, but especially in their current American package, are marked by the same follies, absurdities, and (at times) outright evils that we've seen splattered all over the cultural map. What in theory is simple play becomes hypertrophied, over-dramatized, and ballyhooed spectacle, infantile outpourings of ego. Consider the dramatis personae here: league bureaucracies, millionaire-to-billionaire owners, complaisant city politicians (can't expect owners to pay for their own stadiums), major advertisers, big-name coaches (who have to do double duty as scapegoats, discarded to placate rabid fans), sports writers and TV commentators, sports networks, sports bars, sports doctors, sports lawyers, and steroid-providers.

And then there's the college scene, sometimes a minor-league version of pro-world, sometimes more modest, with complaisant college presidents, easy-grading profs, besotted alumni, deep-pocketed donors, cosseted "scholar-athletes" (many of whom never graduate), screaming student bodies, cheerleading cuties (less pectorally prominent than their sisters in the pros, even as amateur male players are less athletically advanced), and the ever-growing array of "festivals" and league championships, Bowl Games, with their mascots, marching bands, bare-chested, grotesquely Magic-Markered students, tuning up for the alcoholic post-game victory (or defeat) orgy. It looks like too much ado about much too little.

As in other cultural fields, such as the arts, we see recurrent patterns that we've long taken for granted: eye-popping performances (increasingly beyond the capacity of anyone in the audience/stands) hero-worship (e.g., for soccer and basketball stars), glorification of macho violence ("smash-mouth football!" announcers cry out gleefully), politicization (national anthems, players literally wrapping themselves in the flag) and, wherever possible, a dash of "sensitivity" (choked-up claptrap about the various Halls of Fame, Old Timers' Days, video-clips about the childhood tragedies of Olympic athletes, Lou Gehrig's farewell speech at Yankee Stadium, Vin-Scully, and

Joe-Garagiola-style nostalgia,, etc.) Why, one has to ask, in heaven do so many people take games so seriously?

Because it's all about *us*. Anybody can applaud the individual winners of tennis matches, golf tournaments, or figure-skating championships (as well as any particularly fine stroke or move in the course of play); but you don't hail the opposing *team,* nor most of its members, except when an injured player gets up and staggers to the sidelines. It's *our* lads—or gals—out there, playing *our* game (baseball. football, basketball). So, foreign sports take a while to get acclimated: ice hockey still isn't quite there yet, but the US's "miracle on ice" defeat of the Russkies back in 1980 went a long way. Sometimes even losing streaks can create a kind of gallows-humor camaraderie, as with the ill-fated Brooklyn Bums or the Chicago Cubs. Even as community life drifts and dissolves, the culture of games takes us back to something like a tribal world, full of intense, but pointless rivalries and bizarre behavior, (waving towels and rally-monkeys, growling pseudo-Indian war chants, decking or swiping mascots).Yee-HAH!

In any case, there's no use pretending that sports—or any other aspects of culture—are just good, clean fun. While far less lethal than the battles they mimic—putting aside the deaths from luge and skiing accidents, racing car collisions, brain damage in boxing matches, the shooting of referees or own-goal scorers in soccer, and fan stampedes—games display the same dubious stock in trade as other cultural phenomena, such as brutal forms of self-assertive triumphalism. Amusingly enough, one group of critics has proved to be all-too-aware of the dangers of sport—in the most wrongheaded way possible: the Muslim fanatics who freak out over women's skimpy uniforms and in some cases even bar women from male soccer matches (shades of Melina Mercouri in *Topkapi*, lusting over the fleshy horde of Turkish wrestlers).But the liberation sports offer girls and women (not least from stupid religious fixations about "modesty" and other stereotypes peddled by the clergy and blue-nosed males) is a blessing, not a curse.

The dangers, already mentioned, come dolled up in a mix of techno-speak ("nickel back," "small ball," "triangle offense") and venerable sports clichés ("momentum," "in a zone," "till the fat lady sings," "dance with the one that brung you," etc.), dished up by the good buddies of the athletic commentariat, aided by sports "personalities" serving as "color men." There's probably no single dialect of contemporary life more infested with clichés than sports talk. (For a brief dive into this bottomless ocean try http://www.sportscliche.com.) Sports' matey language is a multi-tasker's dream : it establishes the stadium-cred of the speaker, his knowledge of "tradition," his emotional warmth, his regular-guyhood, his down-home savvy and lightly worn expertise. (Sports announcers often apologize, or get twitted, for carelessly dropping polysyllabic words or hoity-toity expressions on the air. Sports talk has to be "natural," i.e., fake.)

Sports talk lays down the guidelines for the viewing experience. It confirms that 1) All games in general, and this game in particular, are extremely *important*, for any number of strategic reasons (storied series, current league standings, later championship match-ups, spotlight on rising/current star), but often just because. (In pro sports every game is a big game, which is why nobody minds "winning ugly.") We watch for the same reason we listen to neighbors argue or rubberneck highway crashes; and the first pitch, jump ball, or kickoff generates a tipsy anticipation , which, alas, often fizzles as the game goes sour and the score gets out of hand. 2) We the spectators are extremely *important*, the *sine qua non* in fact, or one of them, of the whole operation. Our presence and our dollars (though that goes unmentioned) make it happen. Plus, there's the old "twelfth man" theme: the fans as quasi-players, able to turn the game around at any moment. 3) *Everybody* involved is extremely *important*. That includes players too injured to perform, ailing members of the TV crew (hailed from the broadcast booth as they lie in hospital beds or at home convalescing), and recently deceased relatives of anyone at all connected to the game. Sports create cultural community.

No, more, sports are family , blood-brothers on the field, bench, or sidelines, "pardners" calling the game, fans watching it, and even refs calling it (though ideally without intruding), all fused into a temporary clan. Highlights or controverted plays have to be instant-replayed and discussed, like peak moments of artistic masterpieces. In fact, though intellectuals often scorn or ignore them, sports are a microcosm of culture. They include law (the rule book, time-tested, but always open to amendment), commerce (cynics see them as little else, with owners, agents, unions, strikes, etc.), science (sports medicine, kinesiology, biomechanics), strategy and tactics, statistics (handheld computers will soon be as crucial to pro baseball as bats) and lots of esthetics. Under that heading, one could think of athletic contests as *Gesamtkunstwerke*, with elements of dance, instrumental and choral music, jazz (improvisation), video art (JumboTrons), and varying amounts of comedy, tragedy, and melodrama.

As with all cultural spectacles, sports provide us with a quivering mass of folly and nonsense, to which the fans are largely oblivious. Granted, the amount of real evil involved seldom amounts to much—after all, the whole point of sport is its elaborate un-reality, whence its escapist pleasures and (at times) irresistible appeal. One goes to games to be dazzled, not to think or question. But everything the human beast does, even while at play, needs to be suspected.

To take one last example, look at the ubiquitous myth of the hyper-masculine athlete and the hero-worship attendant to it. There's plenty of measurable reality behind this myth, from the splendid physiques (and salaries) of some players to the eager groupies awaiting MLB, NBA, and NFL stars at their hotels, to the frequent rape charges brought against athletes (with a strikingly low rate of conviction).everybody knows about, and many celebrate, this macho glory. Wilt Chamberlain claimed to have slept with 20,000 women; and the beard of Pittsburgh Steeler defensive end Brett Keisel—not the man, the *beard*—had 20,000 fans on Facebook, at least before the Packers won Super Bowl LXV. No wonder gay athletes stay in the closet.

This cult is based on the fame, not the intrinsic sexiness, of the players. And in its broad outlines it's absurd: a bunch of well-muscled monomaniacs trained from childhood to speed through a combination of pointless, repetitive acts. Well, no that's not quite fair. But the public adoration of jocks is more than a little strange, and it sometimes continues long after retirement in the mostly unrelated field of politics (where erstwhile athletes, like other retired businessmen, tend to be deeply conservative—Jim Ryun! Jim Bunning! J.C. Watts!). Actually, no surprise here: it's just culture being crazy again. And perhaps some of the driving force behind the non-stop spread of sports madness is the realization that the physical gifts on display in the stadium are increasingly irrelevant in a society based on brain power.

But really is *anything* in culture based on brain power? As David Hume pointed out in our opening epigraph,

> Tis not contrary to reason to prefer the destruction of the whole world to the scratching of my finger. 'Tis not contrary to reason for me to choose my total ruin, to prevent the least uneasiness of an Indian or person wholly unknown to me. 'Tis as little contrary to reason to prefer even my own acknowledged lesser good to my greater, and have a more ardent affection for the former than the latter.

Passion makes the world go around. Our "rational" brains are tools for getting what the passions want. And just how sordid and stupid and silly many of those desires are can be seen in the bulging annals of culture. The idle proceedings on the field of play, like culture's more serious affairs, show the deep gulf between our professed purposes and what really goes on: a lot of crazy stuff.

Conclusion

There died a myriad,
and of the best, among them,
For an old bitch gone in the teeth,
For a botched civilization,

Charm, smiling at the good mouth,
Quick eyes gone under earth's lid,

For two gross of broken statues,
For a few thousand battered books.

    —Ezra Pound, E.P., Ode Pour L'election de Son Sepulchre (1920)

Looking over the vast Serengeti of culture-talk, from the militantly patriotic right to the tenderly populist left, one is struck by one recurrent note: sentimentality. Self-praise that might sound gauche from a single person becomes jolly good when sung by a full-throated choir. Individual masturbation always seems a little embarrassing and best kept out of sight; but performed *en masse* or in the name of some community ideal, it counts as group ecstasy. One drunken Irishman is a nuisance; hundreds of thousands of them are a glorious St. Paddy's Day. Same thing with May Day parades, July 4th celebrations, the running of the bulls, or the mobs of Shiite maniacs lashing themselves on Ashura. Vaulting to a loftier, long-distance level, classicists can rhapsodize over Greek and Roman antiquity, and biblicists can do the same with ancient Israel, while blithely ignoring the horrors of the cultures in question—nightmarish wars, widespread slavery, near-total misogyny, we-are-the-greatest chauvinism, etc. In the dusk with the light behind her, almost any culture can look fetching.

The situation gets a lot trickier when the groups celebrating themselves are in any major sense oppressed. Thus, we're not supposed to joke about the proliferation of "Studies" programs (Womens, Black, GLBT, Latino/ Latina, etc.), although the paladins and practitioners of such ultra-earnest "disciplines" often—by no means always—trade in scholarly analysis for humorless cheerleading and chanting (There used to be a *Sesame Street* number, dating from 1974, called "There's Nothing We Women Can't Be," with various female puppets cavorting around and singing about their careers. Fine, but there are many things women *can't* be—the same, of course, goes for men—starting with impregnators of other women and successful competitors in male specialties like blood sports and brutal behavior generally.)

Beyond such happy exceptions, the unfortunate fact remains that being mistreated doesn't automatically confer virtue or value. In fact, the odds are that mistreatment will deprive its victims of virtue and value. That is one of the harshest lessons of Primo Levis epoch-making *If This Is a Man* (1947). And oppressed people don't necessarily make good artists—quite apart from the fact that the overwhelming majority of artists and writers *deserve* to be left out of the canon. Speaking of which, there happens, for example, not to be one African-American poet worthy of being called great (in the same league with Whitman or Dickinson, much less Keats or Tennyson). It would be nice if there were world-class and world-famous Chinese skiers, Indian oboists, Russian running backs, Vietnamese astronauts, Japanese jazz composers, Kirghiz historians, and so on; but there aren't—as yet. Arab democracy is going to take a while to develop and mature.

Which doesn't stop the culture-spouters from doing their sentimental thing, for example, in practically everything written or said or depicted in a popular vein about the Confederacy, from the tender-minded meanderings of Shelbv Foote in Ken Burns' *Civil War* series to Virginia Gov. Bob McDonnell's proclamation of April, 2010 as Confederate History Month, which managed not to mention slavery at all. Similar treacly nonsense has long been available, and continues to be bought, sold, and consumed about almost every feature of American history, from the nation's glorious wars, the bulk of which (notably the Civil War and World War I) should never have been fought and did more harm than good. John Boehner and other conservatives shed hot tears over the very "American Dream" (ask the Indians and slaves about that one) they work full time to cancel.

Meanwhile, politically correct liberal politicians, as we learn from WikiLeaks, wink at the massive violations of human rights in Cuba. But that's a familiar pattern, seen in the western leftist cults of Lenin, Stalin (William Duranty, Lillian Hellman et al.) and Mao (Edgar Snow, De Beauvoir and Sartre), the demonization of Trotsky (greetings, Comrade Siqueiros!) and the later romanticization of Castro, Che Guevara, Yassir Arafat, Hugo Chávez, and the like. In their rage at Zionism and the American Empire, some feminists will wink at the unspeakable oppression of women in Muslim countries. Polygyny? Clitoridectomy? Religiously sanctioned wife-beating and withholding of contraceptives? Honor killings? Child marriage? Homophobia? Human rights violations in Gaza, Iran, Pakistan, Saudi Arabia, and everywhere else in the Islamic world? Lots of liberals and still more radicals can live with that. Some things are better not discussed.

Third World good, First World bad! Multicultural leftists, strictly secular to the last man and woman, bow their heads in deep respect before non-western "communities of faith," even though that faith is pre-scientific bosh, and the communities' practices are Stone Age stupid. Writers and critics, like John Le Carré, Hugh Trevor-Roper, or John Berger, who think everything in their own culture is fair game for critics, righteously slammed Salman Rushdie for offending Islam in *The Satanic Verses*. Andres Serran's *Piss Christ* and Chris Ofili's elephant-dung Madonna were cheered as excellent examples of artistic free speech (and why not?) ,but the *Jyllands-Posten* cartoons were condemned by multiculturalists, ranging from Danish prime minister Anders Fogh Rasmussen to the chief rabbi of France Joseph Sitruk to Jack Straw and Bill Clinton, as an unfeeling abomination. P.c. feminist professors inform their classes that while clitoridectomy *is* a bad thing (though some cultural relativists would quarrel even with that), it's basically no different from our cosmetic vaginoplasty and labioplasty, so we westerners have no right to preach to Africans about it. Oh really?

Jesus famously said, Judge not that ye be not judged" (Mt. 7.1); but that will never do. When it comes to culture, "Judge away—call them as you see them, and take your lumps" would be more like it. (Jesus himself seems to agree when he says in John 5.30" As I hear, I judge; and my judgment is just.") Given the enormous amount of violence, folly, cruelty, and self-deception in human life—our genetic marching orders say "Survive!" not "Be nice!"—there really is no rational alternative. Even people in glass houses have the right to throw stones to stop outrageous behavior or at least blow off steam about it. When all's said and done, intellectual grownups *have* to commit themselves to Kant's variously-translated formula for enlightenment: *der Ausgang des Menschen aus seiner selbst verschuldeten Unmündigkeit*: the exiting of humans from the immaturity that's their own fault. A fancy pedigree and a long track record prove next to nothing about the truth of an idea or the value of a practice.

And just as various predatory, aggressive behavioral traits have flourished in society, thanks to their survival-value, the same holds for many of the cruder, crueler features of culture, especially when they get tenderly tarted up to make them more palatable. Perhaps the most familiar example of this is the restaurant experience, where the cooked remains of some hapless beast, a veal calf, say, are served up amid varying degrees of pomp and luxury in what is known as "fine dining." Butchery of a different sort is beautified in the sentimentalized distortion of war, as in Trajan's column, Shakespeare's *Henry V*, Velázquez' *Surrender at Breda*, Lincoln's *Gettysburg Address*, the Arc de Triomphe, the Valle de los Caidos and so on. Other cultural poisons turned into tasty entrees or appetizers would be the childish myths of salvation and divine intervention celebrated in fantastical festivals (Passover, Christmas, Easter, et al.)

Of course, if people want to celebrate, let them—any excuse will do. And better traditional, timeworn hokum like Christmas rather than newfangled hokum like Kwanzaa. But it has to be noted that the factual content of such religio-cultural doings is essentially zero. No, the first-born of Egypt were *not* (thank God) all instantly murdered by the Angel of Death; and three million Hebrews did *not* hike through the Red (or Reed) Sea. Nor did a parthenogenetic baby jet down from heaven to save the world, any more than Jesus' corpse ever came back to life and then flew back into the empyrean.

And then there's the utterly repulsive Eid al-Adha, which Muslims borrowed from the Jews, and which recalls how Abraham bought off his bloodthirsty god by slaughtering a ram. And what better way to both flatter the non-existent Spook credited with this gracious "Just kidding!" episode than by bleeding millions of animals to death? Centuries ago it wasn't surprising that, along with the dumb masses, intelligent adults could go along with such nonsense; but it's time to wake up.

There's no counting the dead-wrong national-regional-local-tribal myths that shape and embellish cultural life, with larger-than-life male figures, historical or otherwise, from epics like The *Shahnameh* (Persian Book of Kings), the *Iliad,* the *Aeneid*, *The Adventures of Amir Hamza*, *The Poem of the Cid* or *The Song of Roland*, the "great men" hymned by Thomas Carlyle, and the 20th century explosion of Supreme Leaders, Helmsmen, *jefes*, and *juntas,* Captains of Industry, Fathers of the Country, and blood-smeared warriors of every stripe, from the endlessly beloved Robert E. Lee to Uncle Ho Chi Minh. Other myths, with lesser, but still weighty, amounts of lies and unreality, include the Free Market Economy (rigged in countless ways). The Glories of Democracy (read Modified Plutocracy), Romantic Love (who needs equality when you've got brainsick worship?), the World-Our-Oyster (dig it out, kill it, gobble it down), the American Dream (the promise of exponentially increasing consumption, where available), The War on Drugs, Paying Your Debt to Society, etc.

Given this gigantic fabric of distortion and delusion, the only sensible way to approach it is with an unrelentingly suspicious eye (and ear and nose and tongue and touch). Cultural memes succeed when they give pleasure; and hence they have to be distrusted. Nietzsche explains this well in *The Anti-christ* (1888):

> The proof by 'pleasure' is a proof *of* pleasure—nothing more; why in the world should it be assumed that *true* judgments give more pleasure than false ones, and that, in conformity to some pre-established harmony, they necessarily bring agreeable feelings in their train?—The experience of all disciplined and profound minds teaches *the contrary*. Man has had to fight for every atom of the truth, and has had to pay for it almost everything that the heart, that human love, that human trust cling to. Greatness of soul is needed for this business: the service of truth is the hardest of all services.—What, then, is the meaning of *integrity* in things intellectual? It means that a person must be severe with his own heart, that he must scorn 'beautiful feelings,' and that he makes every Yea and Nay a matter of conscience!—Belief makes blessed: *therefore, it lies.* (tr. H.L. Mencken, slightly altered.)

Of course, that's not always true; but it's true enough, especially for the addictive-and-destructive elements of culture—consumerism, chauvinism, racism, and so forth. The classic image of this comes from Book VI, 8.13 of Augustine's *Confessions*, where Alypius gets hooked on the gladiatorial games in Milan.

> He, not forsaking that secular course which his parents had charmed him to pursue, had gone before me to Rome, to study law, and there he was carried away incredibly with an incredible eagerness after the shows of gladiators. For being utterly averse to and detesting spectacles, he was one day by chance met by divers of his acquaintance and fellow-students coming from dinner, and they with a familiar violence haled him, vehemently refusing and resisting, into the Amphitheatre, during these cruel and deadly shows, he thus protesting: 'Though you hale my body to that place, and there set me, can you force me also to turn my mind or my eyes to those shows? I shall then be absent while present, and so shall overcome both you and them.' They, hearing this, led him on nevertheless, desirous perchance to try that very thing, whether he could do as he said. When they were come thither, and had taken their places as they could, the whole place kindled with that savage pastime. But he, closing the passage of his eyes, forbade his mind to range abroad after such evil; and would he had stopped his ears also! For in the fight, when one fell, a mighty cry of the whole people striking him strongly, overcome by curiosity, and as if prepared to despise and be superior to it whatsoever it were, even when seen, he opened his eyes, and was stricken with a deeper wound in his soul than the other, whom he desired to behold, was in his body; and he fell more miserably than he upon whose fall that mighty noise was raised, which entered through his ears, and unlocked his eyes, to make way for the striking and beating down of a soul, bold rather than

resolute, and the weaker, in that it had presumed on itself, which ought to have relied on Thee. For so soon as he saw that blood, he therewith drunk down savageness; nor turned away, but fixed his eye, drinking in frenzy, unawares, and was delighted with that guilty fight, and intoxicated with the bloody pastime. Nor was he now the man he came, but one of the throng he came unto, yea, a true associate of theirs that brought him thither. Why say more? He beheld, shouted, kindled, carried thence with him the madness which should goad him to return not only with them who first drew him thither, but also before them, yea and to draw in others (tr. E.B. Pusey).

For Augustine, this was an archetypal tale of temptation and sin, with the same fateful crowd-factor that contributed to his own boyhood crime of robbing a pear tree. Nowadays we might think of bull fights (cock fights for our Latino and Asian brethren) or boxing matches (*Stag at Sharkey's!*) or bellicose soccer matches, and stress, not the sin, but the brutal dumbness of culture. The key to it all is unthinking custom: we do this sort of thing because we do these sorts of things. What could be more natural (Pascal's "second nature") than having tailgate parties before football games, where obese Americans stuff themselves with cooked animal corpses, beer, and booze in preparation for the day's grand athletic rite? Say, isn't that Mike Zuma over there?! Or look at Black Friday throngs (their spirits renewed from watching the Macy's Thanksgiving Day parade') or the Canadian harp seal "harvest;" First Holy Communion processions; the Sweetwater, Texas Jaycees annual Rattlesnake Round-Up; or the blessed Diwali festival (but what if Lord Rama had *not* defeated the demon Ravana? Perish the thought.) Get your crazy culture here!

In the midst of such corporate madness it's hard to keep one's head. Later generations will probably see (some) things more clearly and, for example, ban bull fights altogether (as the Catalonians just did). But in the meantime the cultural spectacles—and the predictable sentimental raptures about them—roll on. The hordes of the dotty faithful collected in Mecca's Masjid al-haram or St. Peter's Square or on the banks of the Ganges; the mobs of the merely spaced-out enthusiasts at rock concerts, political conventions, NASCAR races, or New Year's Eve midnight-howls; of the mostly passive attendees at movies, shows, Sunday sermons, graduations, funerals, etc., and finally of the quasi-unconscious consumers of culture's most common and multiform product (ads)—are all, in one way or another, absorbing lies. They more or less have to be, since that's what's on the menu.

And so? You wanna make sumpin outa that? (as the bullies in my old Brooklyn neighborhood used to say). Indeed, I do (see the whole foregoing screed). Russians like to label uncivilized or boorish people as *nyekulturni*; but that's being way too kind to "culture," which has no necessary connection to good behavior, as evident from the lives of highly cultured men such as Nero.

Cultural activities aren't driven by reason, so it seems fair enough to call much of culture "crazy," both the acts and artifacts humans perpetrate, and the hurrahs accorded them. The examples here are infinite; but one classic case seems to be the repulsive made-up story of the binding of Isaac (or Ishmael for most Muslims). Bad enough as human sacrifice is in itself (nobody asks Sara's or Hagar's opinion), Abraham's obedience is made worse by being celebrated in the daily morning synagogue service, the annual feast of Eid al-Adh (see Chapter I, "The Primal Sin"), and Kierkegaard's loco meditation in *Fear and Trembling*. And then it's constantly touted today by Jews, Christians, and Muslims as a sublime moment of faith, instead of the disgusting throwback to some primitive blood cult that it really is. (Curious how biblical writers keep having to go out of their way to denounce the unthinkable worship of Molech [Lev. 18.21; 20.2-5;2 Kings 23.10, Jer. 32.25, etc.])

Culture no doubt enshrines far more follies than horrors; but in any event it coats them with the patina of age and respectability. Even today Americans still bless the time-honored death penalty. Iranians frown on (and put to death) people accused of *moharebeh,* the unpardonable crime of "waging war against God." Governments all over the world promote the ancient agenda of violent homophobia. And so on. There's no culturally sanctioned custom or belief or representation so insane that it hasn't been, or still is being, put into practice or admired.

Whence my subtitle, "The Sins of Civilization." Certainly "sins" makes more sense when applied to, say, the chauvinism of professional Christian George W. Bush, as opposed to the chauvinism of Francis Scott Key (a long-term V.P. of the American Bible Society). But culture does countless harmful things; and if nothing else, the word itself should be stripped of its traditional halo, aura, and coronet. And while Hanns Johst, the Nazi Poet Laureate and utterly worthless writer cited in my epigraph, himself could serve as an instance of culture's sins (he spent three and a half years in prison after WWII), we can always borrow his celebrated phrase (so often misquoted and misattributed, and however stupidly intended) as a handy comic metaphor. God knows we don't need any more guns; but, given the mind-numbing onrush by the hoplites, peltasts, and chariots of Bad Culture, it's comforting to feel that one can always, figuratively "reach for one's pistol" or press the fire buttons on one's critical joystick, to mow down the bastards and their more or less toxic trash. Crazy, crazy culture, enough already.

www.ingramcontent.com/pod-product-compliance
Lightning Source LLC
Chambersburg PA
CBHW030656270326
41929CB00007B/385